CHANGED

ONCEGAY & DETRANSITIONER STORIES

Published by CHANGED Movement
Redding, California
www.changedmovement.com

Printed in China.

ISBN - 979-8-9888109-1-9

Cover design by Abram Goff

For information about CHANGED Movement,
please visit our website: **www.changedmovement.com**

DISCLAIMER

Every effort has been made to recreate events, locales, and conversations as accurately as possible from the memories of those sharing their stories. In some instances, names of individuals, places, identifying characteristics, and details such as physical properties, occupations, and places of residence have been changed to protect the privacy of individuals.

CREDITS

EDITORS-IN-CHIEF

KEN WILLIAMS

ELIZABETH WONING

DESIGN DIRECTORS

JOANA KIELHORN

BREE STEVENS

SENIOR COPY EDITOR

PAM SPINOSI

COPY EDITORS

CALEB BOGGAN

IVAN SANTOS

JAMIE FREY

LEON JONCK

LINDA HOYER

JESSICA OWENS

JUDY WILLIAMS

CONTRIBUTING WRITERS

MARY BAILEY

CASSANDRA BECK

DARLENE EDSKERUD

NATALIE SHAW

MEGAN SISSON

CHANGED

CVC

CHANGED
MOVEMENT

WE EXIST.
WE EXIST.

CONTENTS

Can a person leave LGBTQ behind?

“CHANGED” began as an effort to highlight the journeys of men and women who have confronted this question in their own lives. Finding themselves with same-sex sexual feelings or gender incongruence, the people featured in this book took paths of self-discovery to find peace.

Today, many question their sexuality alone. Sometimes answers seem beyond reach—you are not alone.

We are a growing community of men and women who have explored the depths of our identities for understanding. We have confronted the pain, rejection, and despair that often accompany the questions, so our approach is sensitive. Compassionate. Genuine.

This is an invitation to go deeper with us. To find meaning in the journey. And to embrace process. We have looked beyond the cultural labels and expectations for lasting fulfillment.

Inside this book are vulnerable, authentic, and sometimes raw accounts of the hope and prosperity all of our journeys offered as we questioned our sexuality and gender identity.

We are changed.

THANK YOU

...to every person who has shared their story for the creation of this book.
Your courage and vulnerability are remarkable.

BRIAN BARLOW

DESERT STREAM MINISTRIES
desertstream.org

"

I heard about a program that helps individuals overcome unwanted same-sex attraction. It offered me freedom and clarity.

BRIAN BARLOW

I grew up hiding my same-sex attractions from others because I felt that it wouldn't be right for me to act on them. But after college, I sought out a counselor and talked about my same-sex feelings and resulting internal conflict for the first time. After meeting with me for a few months, he looked at me and said, "Well, maybe you should go to the gay bars in Chicago. That might be how God created you." I was 21, and his response devastated me.

Early in my life, I'd been ridiculed by family members and peers for behaviors they believed were feminine, but my defense was I didn't have any homosexual experiences. I was looking for someone to confirm my belief and hope that this was not my identity. Instead, the counselor I met with held the door open to homosexuality and said there was no hope for change. So, I acted on that out of desperation for connection and began to identify as gay in the gay community.

I am more alive than I could have ever imagined.

This opened a door to sexual behaviors that I didn't have peace in pursuing and emotional and relational confusion. The despair I felt further disintegrated my ability to relate as a whole person, and I became overly sexualized, separating me from my family, faith community, and friends. I became void of an identity, following after anyone who paid attention to me. I was vulnerable to abuse by others because I was desperate for love and had no boundaries.

I read faith-based books that told the stories of other people who had unwanted same-sex attraction. Then I heard about a church that offered a program to help individuals overcome unwanted same-sex attraction, so I enrolled in the program. It offered me freedom and clarity. For the first time in my life, I had language to describe what I was experiencing.

Afterwards, I connected with more people whom I could trust with my story and who helped counsel me through it. I pursued help and encouragement through groups that met to process same-sex attractions. Emotionally healthier, I began to experience attraction for women. My same-sex desires no longer captivated me and consumed my thoughts. My confidence grew as I began to live out my God-given gender identity, fully male.

It was then that I met my wife at church. The clarity I received in my journey to wholeness made it possible to step into this relationship. We married six months later. 11 years later, we have four children.

For several years we owned and operated a faith-based art gallery in Palm Springs, California. There we built relationships with individuals in the LGBTQ community. The arts gave us common ground to talk about faith and identity. Individuals would come back again and again, as we shared our story of hope. My life today may seem impossible to some, but I am more alive than I could have ever imagined.

"

There was no manipulation or shame, just unconditional love.

LIZ FLAHERTY

My family moved to a small California town when I was young. I faced a lot of rejection growing up there for multiple reasons: one was that I was overweight and the other that I was a Christian. Attempting to fit in, I continually sought out romantic relationships, smoked pot, and abused alcohol. With plummeting self-worth, I gave myself to any guy willing to give me attention.

During high school, I found my relationships with men to be shallow, and I became calloused towards them. I found my relationships with women to be much deeper and more fulfilling. I'd experienced same-sex attraction from a young age, but hadn't talked to anyone about it.

One night as I sat with my friends, I had what I believed was my grand epiphany: I was a lesbian. I thought the pieces of my puzzle were coming together.

In college, I joined an LGBTQ community and separated myself completely from my religious upbringing. I believed I had been liberated and could pursue what I knew was best for me. Even with this new "liberation," I was still experiencing tremendous pain and depression, which led to medicating myself.

One afternoon as I was high, I became greatly aware of the severity of my depression and feeling of disconnection from God. I began to pray, "I'm not sure if it's okay to talk to you when I'm high, but I can't get myself out of this." Suddenly, I was overwhelmed with the feeling that God truly loved me. For the next few days, I tried to resume my regular routine; however, when I went to smoke again, I felt like I was going to die. I didn't want to quit, but eventually I realized that, clearly, I was to follow a different path going forward.

After this experience, I renewed my focus on my faith in God, including how it related to my sexuality. And even in the midst of all that, I continued to experience same-sex attraction.

After searching to understand my same-sex attraction, I was introduced to a sexual wholeness program that emphasized finding your true identity. It was led by a married couple who had walked through similar struggles. The group met once a week and formed a loving environment where we could open up, receive encouragement, and seek healing. These leaders let us be our messy selves, all the while helping us to grow. There was no manipulation or shame, just unconditional love. In that season of my life, I grew to understand where my desires and attractions came from and how to get deep emotional needs met in an appropriate and effective way.

These days, same-sex attraction no longer drives me. I know who I am and have a tremendous amount of peace and joy. I've been married to a wonderful man for 19 years now. I'm no longer in the painful cycle of trying to fulfill my needs through lesbian relationships.

LIZ G. FLAHERTY
lizgflaherty@gmail.com

LIZ FLAHERTY

DREW BERRYESSA

A LIVING LETTER MINISTRIES
alivingletter.org

“

No one there was trying to coerce me into changing my behavior, but they helped me pursue a healthy heart and lifestyle.

DREW BERRYESSA

I lived in what felt like a secret prison of hopelessness and helplessness. I was addicted to pornography and masturbation, and I had a really hard time making friends. I also dealt with same-sex attraction and felt extremely internally conflicted and frustrated about it. I had no idea what to do with my struggles.

At my lowest point, I was in despair and had no hope that things could change. I started to believe that gay love was better than no love at all, and I entered into a gay relationship. For a few months it felt fulfilling, but then I quickly realized it wasn't what others had made it out to be.

Realizing that even that relationship wouldn't meet my heart's desire or satisfy me, I considered suicide. I saw no way forward, but I didn't go through with it.

I wanted to have a family someday, to be married to a woman, and have kids although I honestly didn't think it would be possible for me. And I always had a deep feeling that same-sex attraction was not what was best for me. I struggled to reconcile my feelings and my faith. These were the two main motivators for me to pursue change.

There were many things that helped my process, including an album of a worship leader who shared his story of coming out of homosexuality. It was the first time I'd ever heard a testimony like it, and it gave me hope. There were also books of others' stories of leaving gay life that encouraged me.

I then joined a program that offered specific counseling and pastoral care for people who struggled with their sexuality. No one there was trying to coerce me into changing my behavior, but they helped me pursue a healthy heart and lifestyle, which then led me to change my behavior, as well. The people there encouraged me and helped me see who I really was. That meant letting go of the ways the rejection, abuse, and struggle had affected my view of myself.

Now I have been married for 20 years to my wife, and I am the father of three beautiful daughters. Those are two roles that I never thought I would be able to have. I now get to experience them every single day, and it's amazing.

I have an immense number of healthy, supportive friendships, and I have had reconciliation with each of my family members whom I felt isolated from in the past. I'm happy, successful, and excited about life.

I could have never imagined the life that I am living now. I am in a thriving marriage with my wonderful wife, and we together are watching our three daughters grow into incredible young women. Every day, whether special or mundane, is a gift I never thought I would have. These gifts are mine because I had the opportunity to heal and transform: an opportunity I never would have had if the help I found had been withheld from me. I am so grateful that was not the case!

BREE STEVENS

CHANGED MOVEMENT
changedmovement.com

"

Counseling helped me revisit the sexual assault, which I discovered was linked to all my health issues, PTSD, and same-sex attraction.

BREE STEVENS

When I was fifteen, I was blindsided by sexual assault. For years afterward I battled depression, self-hatred, self-harm, pornography and masturbation, fear of men, and PTSD. I was terrified of revisiting the incident, so I suppressed it and went on medication to cope with my health and psychological issues.

In college I met a girl who, to this day, is my best friend. Our friendship developed quickly, and we became extremely close. Although we'd suffered different forms of abuse, we became the answer to each other's pain, and the emotional intimacy we shared turned sexual.

I could never fully resonate with identifying as lesbian or bisexual, yet I couldn't deny that I was in a same-sex relationship with my best friend. I hated what we were doing in secret, and I never found lasting fulfillment. The escape I sought from my sexual trauma by being with her was short-lived and only reinforced the disconnect I felt toward men. I convinced myself it was just a phase that would go away on its own, but three years later we were still stuck in a secret that was increasingly hard to hide. I actually felt empty and more isolated than before we became friends.

Today, I feel whole.

The turning point for me happened when I woke up next to her one morning and saw two versions of my life flash before my eyes. In one future, I saw myself living an openly gay life and married to her; behind me was a completely severed relationship with my family. In the next future, I saw us standing beside each other and married, but not to each other. Our husbands, kids, and families surrounded us. We were in love with our husbands and more satisfied with them than we ever were with each other, and my relationship with my parents was restored. In that moment I heard Jesus say to me, "You can be with your best friend forever. Whichever way you choose, I promise you, I will never leave you. But, if you choose a relationship with her, you will leave Me." I couldn't bear the thought of leaving Jesus. I knew He was telling me the truth.

So I chose. She chose. We both wanted the second future, so we asked people in our church for help. The thought of opening up about our closeted relationship was terrifying, but they embraced us. I got pastoral counseling and read books about finding freedom in my sexuality. Counseling helped me revisit the sexual assault, which I discovered was linked to all my health issues, PTSD, and same-sex attraction. Within months, my PTSD symptoms dissipated, I went off medication, and the sexual draw I had toward her began to change. She went through her own healing process too, and we've been healthy and free for nine years now. The sexual tension and codependency are gone. We love our friendship this way.

Today, I feel whole. I feel safe around men again, and it is no longer difficult to look them in the eyes. I am even looking forward to dating guys, something I have not felt in years. I love my body now and feel deeply restored.

"

I had been wanting to pursue change for quite some time before the tragedy at Pulse happened.

ANGEL COLON

My life before I pursued change in my sexuality was what I would call "a hot mess." Lonely, empty, unhappy, shackled, and unloved were the ways I felt for eight years after I came out. The more unhappy I was, the worse it got. My life was so consumed by gay sexuality, drugs and liquor that I wouldn't give the time of day to my family. Having been raised in a strong Christian home, I felt a deep conflict between what I had known to be good and right, and the life I was living.

I woke up hungover on June 11th, 2016, after a night of drinking and drug use. That evening my friends and I went to Pulse, a club in Orlando. At 2:02 a.m. everything changed. While saying our goodbyes, we heard a big POP! I dropped my drink, realizing the sounds were gunshots. As we ran, I was shot several times and fell down, pulling my friends with me. Struggling to stand back up, I felt a foot step behind my left leg and heard a loud snap which resulted in my left femur breaking. I couldn't move or even feel my legs, so I covered my head and stayed still. What followed was chaos all around me. I started comforting the lady lying next to me, whispering to her to pretend to be dead. I looked at her and heard a loud shot. As her eyes shut, I couldn't believe I just witnessed her death. I was terrified I would be next. Feeling the shooter behind me, I uttered what I thought would be my last prayer. Even in that terrible moment, the peace and hope of God flooded me. I heard a loud shot and felt my body jump up and down. I thought I was dead. After several minutes, I started hearing cop radios. I raised my hands, calling out: "Please come get me! I'm alive!"

I can now say I know what true happiness is, what true love is, and most importantly, what true peace is.

I had been wanting to pursue change for quite some time before the tragedy at Pulse happened. I missed my faith, and I missed feeling true peace and happiness. I had started praying for God to do something to change my life. As I recovered, the support of my pastors became a lifeline. I found that I could talk to them about anything without judgment or rejection and receive counsel and help. Since they earned my trust, I've been able to embrace crucial help and resources to aid me in rediscovering my life and faith. I'm still recovering but very grateful I am here today. My life now is a complete 180 from the life I had before.

Feeling empty and lonely inside was slowly destroying me, but I can now say I know what true happiness is, what true love is, and most importantly what true peace is.

ANGEL COLON

Orlando Pulse Nightclub Shooting Survivor

FEARLESS IDENTITY
fearlessidentity.co

“

I encountered the living Jesus as the only one who could save me from myself.

ANDREW FRANKLIN

In 2006, I was fresh out of college, pursuing a musical theater career in New York City. I was gay-identified and sexually addicted. Relationship after relationship failed and hookup after hookup just made me feel bad about myself and the choices I was making.

My lowest point came after a party that I had gone to one night with a few friends. I had blacked out, but I found out that I had disrespected my friends in really bad ways and tried to coerce another guy into having sex with me. I realized that seeking love my own way was making me more than disappointed; it was making me dangerous.

Desperate for somewhere to turn, I unpacked an old Bible from under my bed. There, I encountered the living Jesus as the only one who could save me from myself. When I bowed down before him in my bedroom, I heard Him speak to me, “Andrew, I'm not mad at you.” In a moment, my shame was replaced with hope.

> **In a moment, my shame was replaced with hope.**

A friend recommended I talk with a pastoral caregiver, who had also followed Jesus away from gay identity, and I met with him weekly for the next several years. Through individual counseling, support groups, and reading powerful books from others who had left LGBTQ to follow Jesus, God healed the real places of pain in my heart: the bullying I endured as a kid and my feelings of abandonment from my dad who had been emotionally unavailable to me and ultimately committed suicide. I had no idea how much these and other factors were impacting my view of God, myself, and other men, but God faithfully showed me my real needs and met them, all while setting me free from my addiction to same-sex encounters as a way of escape.

Today I am no longer sexually addicted. I've been sober for 17 years. I've found that having healthy, platonic relationships with men is much more fulfilling than having sexual encounters with them.

Several years after making these life changes, I met a woman from my church who is now my wife. We've been married for 11 years and have four children. I have crazy, amazing children and a fulfilling marriage, and I'm learning how to best love her and make her feel safe and come alive. I'm a pastor and church planter now, and I meet with many individuals and help them. My life looks drastically different than it did 17 years ago, and I'm so thankful for that.

ANDREW FRANKLIN

KRIS OLSEN

COMING OUT AGAIN
comingoutagain.org

"

I needed a counselor—someone who could help me unravel the deep emotions.

KRIS OLSEN

I was attracted emotionally to other girls in junior high school. In my late teens, I started feeling physically attracted to girls. I never gay-identified, as I didn't like the feelings and wanted them to go away. I was frustrated, had no idea where the attraction was coming from, and wanted nothing to do with it.

In my early 30s, I had a powerful encounter with Jesus and received him as my Savior. I thought that as a Christian, I would not experience same-sex attraction anymore. But, although I wasn't acting on it at all, it did not go away. I'm a member of the LPGA and was so focused on my career that attractions faded to the background.

I enjoy my freedom and am happy.

About ten years after becoming a Christian, while in a business meeting, I looked across the room and made eye contact with a woman. I was immediately attracted to her, and I could see in her eyes that she was extremely attracted to me, too. I didn't want to pursue anything with her, so I resolved to keep my distance.

A couple of months later in another business meeting, she sat down next to me. She asked how I was doing, and I ended up unloading all of my work-related frustrations and struggles on her. She offered to help me because she'd had similar experiences, so I agreed. We struck up a friendship, which became a relationship, and I entered into the world of lesbian sexuality. She was practically my dream girl, but all along, I felt unsettled about it and very internally conflicted.

She wasn't a Christian, and I was. One day as we sat in my car talking, I mentioned a biblical concept that applied to our topic of conversation. I said, "There's this Scripture in the Bible that says...." I barely finished when she turned to me and said, "Shut up! I'm so tired of hearing about Jesus. If you mention Him one more time, I'm out of this car and you'll never see me again."

Suddenly, I knew I was at a crossroads of choosing my faith or her. In that moment, I chose my faith.

It was the hardest decision I had ever made, and I knew I needed serious help to work through it. I needed more than just reading Scripture; I needed a counselor—someone who could help me unravel the deep emotions from a faith-based perspective. I ended up joining a Christian ministry program where I gained understanding about where my same-sex feelings had come from. I also attended a conference and read a couple of books on the topic of transforming unwanted same-sex attraction. All of these things were healing for me.

Today, I'm no longer attracted to women, and I have attraction toward men. I'm currently single, enjoy my freedom and am happy with being released from the intense conflict in my soul over my sexuality.

"

I learned how to be a good friend to guys (hard at first) and to love a woman, whom I married. Best choice ever.

ANDREW COMISKEY

My freedom from the domination of homosexuality began with a revelation of the Cross: God's radical self-giving. God gave all and all He asked is that I give Him all. That took time. Young and sexually charged, I found giving up "gay stuff" hard. I knew deep down that my ways were destructive, but I had not enough traction with Christians to discover how divine Love could surpass my feelings. I volleyed between gay and Christian culture for a while before I "got" the Cross. Surrender to Jesus made the difference.

God invited me to dig deeper into why I was at odds with my masculinity.

Second, God showed me I was created in His image—a man intended for a woman. That is an unquestionable truth, but my Bible-toting world stressed what I should not do sexually rather than who I was as God's gendered guy. That invited me to dig deeper into why I was at odds with my masculinity and to get on with the business of relating to women. Gender reconciliation became a priority in my thinking and in my daily decisions. I learned how to be a good friend to guys (hard at first) and to love a woman, whom I married. Best choice ever.

I also learned that unless I was rooted in a dynamic community of faith, I would be sucked back into perverting my need for love. I grew to love the real presence of Jesus in His Word and saints, in music, and in our efforts to create a home for Him. As we gathered at the first Vineyard Church in Los Angeles, He deepened authentic worship. There my fiancé and I began to gather with gay-identified persons whom we helped to know Jesus. Together we discovered His strength perfected in weakness. That became the basis for Living Waters, a group I still run as a Catholic in my parish; our groups now flow out to every continent (desertstream.org). My well-being is bound up in helping make the broken body of Christ beautiful for Jesus.

ANDREW COMISKEY

DESERT STREAM MINISTRIES
desertstream.org

DAVID REECE

"

I could have come out and said, "I'm going to live a gay lifestyle," but I didn't want it.

DAVID REECE

From the time I was age three to seventeen, my life was marked by addiction to pornography, same-sex porn, unhealthy relationships, confused identity and sexual abuse. I lived a duplicitous life with a lot of behind-closed-doors behavior. I seemed like a great kid. No one suspected I was in pain, but I was lonely and confused.

My cousin molested me from age three to sixteen. From the age of four, I was attracted to other boys. In high school, I was addicted to porn and had encounters with other boys, so I thought maybe I was gay. But when a close friend came out, I knew it wasn't what I wanted and made a conscious decision not to go down that path.

I have freedom and clarity.

In college, I didn't act out but used gay pornography to comfort myself in my loneliness and brokenness. When I met my wife in 2008, she was the first person I was honest with about my lifelong addiction to porn and same-sex attraction. I was very attracted to her, but I didn't know how to reconcile that with the conflict raging within me.

In 2010 we married, and I took my porn addiction into our marriage. By the second year of marriage things got really rough. I knew I desperately needed help. One night a friend told me about a program he was in that was helping him to experience healing and to understand his sexuality; he encouraged me to check it out. That was the turning point for me. Right away I started counseling sessions that helped me get out of pain and confusion and understand that just because I was molested at three didn't mean I was gay. Then I went through a 21-week program directed at sexual brokenness and relational trauma. In 2015, through counseling and the 21-week program, I got freedom and healing from the roots that had been causing all my pain and sexual confusion, and it's been an acceleration ever since.

Before I walked out of same-sex attraction, I only knew fake happiness. Today my life is crazy good and full of joy. For the first time in my life, I have freedom and clarity, and things keep getting clearer every day. I'm finally genuinely connected to myself and others, I have confidence in relationships and in myself, and everything is so much clearer now.

There is no doubt in my mind that if I had not had access to the counseling, books, and programs I went through, it would have been soul-crushing. I could have come out and said, "I'm going to go live a gay lifestyle," but I didn't want it. I didn't know what to do, and I was in despair. I had so many thoughts of suicide and so much darkness surrounding my life because it was so lonely and depressing. If I had not had the opportunity to pursue the healing and wholeness I was longing for, I would be dead today.

"

Counseling saved my life because it gave me encouragement and a totally confidential space to share everything.

KEN WILLIAMS

I was the scrawniest boy in every class from kindergarten through high school, and I had great difficulty in keeping up with or fitting in with the boys. At eight years old while playing outside, some boys exposed me to hard-core gay pornography and touched me sexually. I was desperately confused by the experiences and, from there, lived with overwhelming shame that I kept hidden for the next ten years.

On my walks home from school, male peers yelled out slurs at me like "faggot" and "homo." So, I feared male social interactions—the locker room, recess, and lunch break. I distanced myself from most boys—definitely the rough and tumble ones—and canceled the masculinity around me as best I could. To me it was inappropriate, rude, and ungodly.

But my need for masculine connection grew stronger, the more I pushed it away. While I rejected the brash, masculine stereotypical guy, I actively sought out whichever male peer I deemed to be strong who was also kind. If he showed me attention or affirmation, I felt valuable. If I could have his undivided attention, I was okay for the minute.

By middle school, I was experiencing same-sex attraction, which caused me to hate myself all the more because I didn't want to have those desires. I developed one unhealthy friendship after the next through my teens, trying to find myself in each young man. Codependency, plain and simple. But no matter how much time or attention I received from a guy, it never was enough, even in the times it turned sexual. My "friend" would head home for the evening, and I was lost again. Obsessed. Depressed.

When I was 17, I felt so hopeless that I started planning my suicide. I just couldn't imagine fighting the same-sex desires my whole life or bearing the weight of the loneliness and self-hatred I felt on a daily basis.

Scared that I would actually end my life, I finally told my parents about the depths of my pain and asked to see a Christian counselor. As a minor, I began seeing him weekly. Those five years of counseling saved my life because it gave me encouragement and a totally confidential space to share everything—all the shame over sexual encounters, pent up anger from being bullied, feelings of inadequacy, codependent fixations, and loneliness. He recommended that I join a support group, and there I realized for the first time that I wasn't alone. The group pointed me to books, which I devoured, containing examples of people whose sexual feelings had changed over time. The books also helped me discover underlying issues contributing to my sexual identity confusion.

I then attended a ministry school and my addictions to pornography and masturbation, as well as my bent toward codependent fixation, dramatically waned. There, I began to experience God as affirming, forgiving, and a kind Father who could be trusted. These were attributes of God I'd not known before.

In time, I was not sexually aroused by men anymore. I started to notice a young lady in my church and found myself being captivated by the sight and thought of her. Months later, I asked her out, and we were married less than a year later. My wife is my closest and most treasured companion, and we've been married since 2006. We have a great sex life and four children together.

Today, I have peace. I'm blessed with plenty of friends, and I feel known and valued by even the men in my community. I enjoy my life. None of that was true before.

KEN WILLIAMS

CHANGED MOVEMENT
Co-founder
changedmovement.com

AMANDA DENNIS

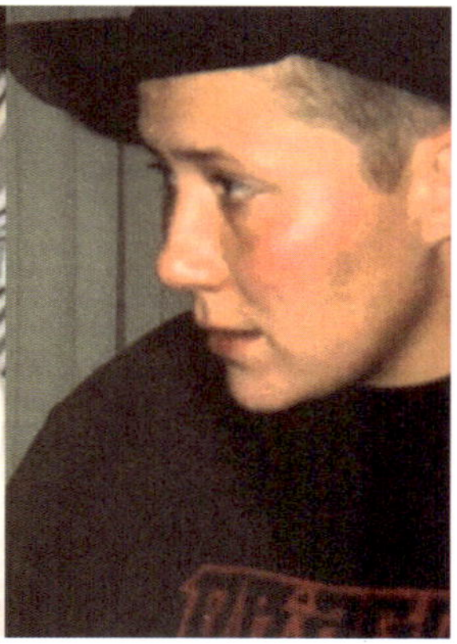

"

It's not about religion telling me what to do; it's something that's coming from the inside out.

AMANDA DENNIS

I used to be a serial dater. I identified as a lesbian, and I had one relationship after another. Plus, I had problems with addictions to drugs and alcohol, and I was violent and angry.

When I came to faith in Christ, I no longer wanted to feel same-sex attraction. Of course, many people said I shouldn't have those attractions because of what the Bible says about homosexuality, and I agreed with them. I didn't feel like I should have those attractions to other women, either. I certainly didn't want them.

My heart's coming alive in a new way.

So I found myself isolating from Christian women, and it caused me a lot of depression and anxiety. I didn't feel free in my relationships, and I was falling into an emotionally dependent relationship with any female I got close to. It went beyond sexual attraction; the pull I felt towards women had a lot to do with my desire for closeness emotionally.

When feelings of isolation and depression became severe, I reached out to a lady who worked at a ministry and had left a lesbian lifestyle herself. She walked with me through my process for a couple of years and her story gave me hope.

Later, I found another ministry that helps people deal with attractions that they don't want. I went through three of their paid programs, and they were extremely helpful for me. They equipped me with a handful of books with stories of people with same-sex attractions and how they dealt with them. Those stories touched me because they showed me I wasn't alone and gave me practical ideas for how to handle my attractions.

Counseling was also really important for me because it helped me with the battle in my mind. I had a lot of unhealthy thought patterns about who I am specifically as a woman. I was constantly comparing myself and creating paralyzing insecurities. Therapy helped me learn how to get rid of those thoughts.

Today, I don't have to be concerned about being around women. In the past I couldn't see the good in another woman without latching on to her or diminishing who I was as a woman. But now, I have deeper relationships with women and am secure in myself. As a declaration and celebration that God transforms all who surrender to Him, my husband and I decided to get married on the first day of June in 2024. I realize that marriage is not the end-all, be-all goal of healing, and I do not consider it a sign that I have "arrived," but this I do know: it is because of Jesus that I can be attracted to and love a man. I do not need to pursue women like a man, but in more profound ways, I am allowing my heart to be safe and secure in the love of Jesus through my husband's love and care for me.

I used to dress like a man and talk like a man. And it's funny because now I actually desire to be feminine in ways that I never had before, and I love it. My heart's coming alive in a new way. It's not about a religion telling me what to do, it's something that's coming from the inside out. I feel like God is changing me on the inside, and it's being shown on the outside.

"

I realized I was never going to get the identity or affirmation from any of the men I was with. I never felt more alone.

DEAN GREER

I was very insecure as a boy. When I was eight, I was introduced to child sex play by a male friend. My emotional longings became sexualized, and I began longing for more sexual encounters. I wasn't very athletic and was ostracized in school, called names like "gay" and "fag." I decided that it must be true because after all, I was sexually attracted to other males.

I knew my family and community wouldn't condone a gay identity, so I hid it and moved away to join the Navy. Suddenly, what had been a source of shame was celebrated. I was popular and no longer the ostracized man. I went from one gay relationship to another.

After about two years, I was diagnosed with HIV on a ship-wide screening. It was 1989, and I was 21. I was told I had 10 more years left. It forced me to reexamine my life, and I realized I was never going to get the identity or affirmation from any of the men I was with. All they wanted was the sex. I never felt more alone in the world.

I'm so grateful I didn't settle for less than what I hoped was possible.

I went home and told my family I was gay and HIV positive. I anticipated rejection, but they were very loving. I met with a family friend who had also experienced same-sex attraction. He was now married with three kids and no longer living homosexually. I believed that I was born the way I was. But I resolved to give God an opportunity to show me a different way forward.

I went to a therapist who helped me understand how my childhood had distorted the development of my identity as a man. I joined faith-based support groups and programs that gave me tools for living an empowered life. Reading books also gave me practical ways to walk out my new identity. Several of them gave me strength and clarity.

With my homosexual past and HIV, I never thought a woman would want me or that I'd ever have children. I've been married now for 27 years to my beautiful wife, Crystal. And my son Jeremiah turned 16 this year. I'm so grateful I didn't settle for less than what I hoped was possible.

DEAN GREER

DESERT STREAM MINISTRIES
desertstream.org

STEPHEN THOMAS

STEPHEN THOMAS CONSULTING
stephenthomasconsulting.com

"

I believe that God's answer to my prayer, "Please remove this from me," was, "Here's an opportunity to stop hiding. Would you like to take it?"

STEPHEN THOMAS

I grew up in a Christian family. My parents were able to pass their faith on to me, and for as long as I can remember, I have followed Jesus. Simultaneously, though, I experienced emotional woundings in my childhood. Those woundings led to a pornography addiction at age seven and grew into a struggle with same-sex attraction.

My parents' financial struggles resulted in frequent oversight by my older siblings and many hours alone watching television. Television exposed me to sexuality and made me more vulnerable to porn exposure and its allure. I experienced a lot of shame from viewing porn because the unspoken message was that sex is bad until you're married. I hid this and felt that something was wrong with me. I believed I was "a pervert."

At age eight, I attended a new school where I was bullied. I would come home and cry to my parents, asking them to take me out of that school. One significant event was being the only boy in my class not invited to a birthday party. I believed I was left out because I wasn't as good at sports and because something was wrong with my personality. I learned to isolate because I didn't want to experience the pain of being picked on and made fun of. Looking back, I can see that porn was an escape from the loneliness and boredom I was experiencing as a result of my isolation.

During puberty at age 12, I had increased curiosity about the men in the porn I was viewing. I noticed that they represented guys that the girls wanted. I remember feeling that I could never be like them and that they were more masculine than me. At one point, I realized that I had become fixated on the men and, because I was already in an aroused state, I became confused about my attraction toward them. I remember saying to myself, "Oh no, I've made myself gay."

I hid these feelings and attractions because they only added to all the insecurity I was already carrying. During college, my pornography use grew into engaging in sexual encounters with men. Fortunately, my faith was still alive, and I intrinsically knew that this unwanted attraction had to do with my insecurities and pain and was not my true identity. Many times, I cried out, asking God to take it away, but He didn't. Instead, He gave my parents and brother dreams about me regarding what was going on in my life. I believe that God's answer to my prayer, "Please remove this from me," was, "Here's an opportunity to stop hiding. Would you like to take it?" Eventually, I responded and began to build a life without secrets.

I started receiving counseling, joined some small groups and engaged in accountability with my brother from whom I didn't hide anything. Two years into that process, I met a woman who I felt very attracted to, so much so that I wanted to enter into a relationship with her. I had the vision and clarity to leave pornography and hookups behind and have not engaged in those behaviors for over 16 years. Today, we are very happily married and have three children together. I feel confident in myself as a man and have been able to give up being fixated on the idea that other men are better than me.

"

I'm indebted to the programs and counselors that helped me get my life back.

CECIL JACKMAN

I was raised in church. Growing up, I bonded with girls more than boys. My grandma was also my biggest love. I didn't bond with my dad. He was a workaholic and abusive, both verbally and physically.

I was sexually abused from a young age: raped at age four by my babysitter in the bathtub. I felt that if I had been a girl, she wouldn't have done that to me. At school, my third grade teacher's aide told the entire class I was a homosexual and explained in detail what that meant. My nickname became "Cecil the Homo" through the eighth grade. In eighth grade, I was fondled by my male teacher. Not being good at sports involving a ball, I was constantly made fun of in gym class, which further ostracized me from boys my age.

In college, I became a regular at the adult bookstore. I became addicted to hardcore gay porn and masturbation, though I had no relations until I was 26.

I decided I would be a good, celibate, gay Christian man. I decided to work as hard as I could for God so He'd free me. But change never happened. So after a couple of years of serving in every ministry I could find, I became convinced God hated me.

At 26, I ran into a gay cousin I hadn't seen in years. The next night, we went to a gay bar. I felt free. I was with guys like me. But while I sat there having a beer, I felt like God said, "What are you doing here?" So I stood up, told my cousin I had to go home, and left. The next week, I felt that same conviction to leave, but this time I drank my beer, partied and had sex with another man.

I had only technically come out for two months, but I hit bottom fast. One night when I was driving home from a night of gay clubbing, I realized I wasn't feeling the sense of connection to God anymore. It left me feeling alone and empty. I was desperate and put myself into a rehab program in New York. The pastor there said he could help me.

I never imagined I could feel this much hope.

It wasn't an easy process, and I wanted to quit at times. But I was at my end and determined to press forward. I met with a counselor every day. We worked through different things like forgiveness. It was difficult, but I eventually felt much freer. I also roomed with two heterosexual men and bonded with men in a healthy way for the first time in my life.

The change wasn't overnight, but it was continual. Seven years later, I married a woman named Christine. Today, we are blessed to have three kids and two grandsons.

I'm indebted to the programs and counselors that helped me get my life back. After the trauma and despair, I never imagined I could feel this much hope about the future.

CECIL JACKMAN

CHANGED MOVEMENT
changedmovement.com

“

Six years after leaving the gay lifestyle, I met my wife, Amanda. I love being a husband and “Daddy” to our three children.

JIM DOMEN

I never imagined that I would enter the homosexual lifestyle after being raised in a God-fearing home and accepting Christ at age seven. However, after I graduated from college, I was so desperate to love and be loved that I didn’t care that my partner was HIV and hepatitis C positive.

Nonetheless, when I lost all my worldly possessions on June 8, 2002, God changed my life forever. I heard God’s voice telling me to come back to Him. I told God, “I’m yours again,” and I began to realize that His strength is made perfect in my weakness. The next morning, I found $5.00 on the sidewalk. The second I picked it up, I heard God say, “I took care of the Israelites in the desert; I’ll take care of you in yours.”

I am no longer desperate to love and be loved.

This was the first of many miracles that began my journey of transformation. I pursued years of professional therapy, as well as programs through Desert Stream Ministries (Cross Current and Living Waters). These tools were instrumental when it came to understanding same-sex attraction and walking in freedom from homosexuality. Although the counseling and programs never promised I would be freed from temptation, they provided tools to pursue a way of life using God’s design for sexuality.

Then in 2005, I began dating! I remember thinking, “Wow, God. The plumbing you designed for the opposite sex is working!” Although I dated many women, I never thought I’d find a wife because I was 34 years old and “the good ones were already taken.” That’s when I gave up my quest and told God I would focus on His kingdom. Yet God had something better planned for me…

Six years after leaving the gay lifestyle, I met my wife, Amanda, “God’s gift from heaven.” We were married in 2009, and five years later God blessed us with our daughter, Aliah, whose name in Hebrew means “ascending to God.” In September 2016, Amanda gave birth to our son, Ryker, whose name means “strong leader.” In 2018, our third child, Asher Elizabeth, was born — and I couldn’t be more blessed.

I love being a husband and “Daddy” to our three children and am no longer desperate to love and be loved.

JIM DOMEN

NOT A MISTAKE
notamistake.com

DAREN MEHL

MADE FREE MINISTRIES

madefreeministries.com

"

God healed my mind and my heart, and then my behavior and sexual attractions changed.

DAREN MEHL

In my early twenties, I attempted to live as a celibate gay, but that all changed the night I was raped at a party. The trauma threw me into a spiral of same-sex encounters. To avoid HIV, I moved in with my boyfriend and settled into a monogamous relationship. For nearly a decade, although I looked happy on the outside, I lived in constant inner turmoil and stress because I knew my homosexual behavior wasn't who I was. I did my best to ignore my inner voice, but doing so came at a high cost to my personal peace and conscience.

All that began to change the night I was invited to a prayer service and told a friend about my inner battle. Deep down I knew I hadn't been created gay but couldn't reconcile why I had same-sex attraction. My friend prayed for me, and for the first time in my life, I saw clearly that my issue was sexual addiction, not sexual orientation. That night, my hope was restored in my long-lost dream to marry a woman and have a family. Right then and there, I asked God to end my same-sex relationship because I knew I couldn't do it myself, and I asked Him to arrange it so I could marry a particular woman. When I got home that night, my boyfriend abruptly ended our relationship, and soon I was dating and eventually married the exact woman I had prayed for.

While this set me on a course towards personal peace and fulfillment, even as a happily married man, I could not break my secret addiction to gay porn. Despite my best efforts, I cheated on my wife with another man. In an instant, instead of feeling fulfilled and satisfied, I felt dead. I thought I'd lost it all—my wife, my unborn son, my best friends—but by a miracle of mercy and love, my wife took me back.

I now see other men as potential friends, not sexual partners.

Desperate for help to get free from gay porn, I pursued spiritual counseling. Over the next year, through the help of many powerful books and resources, weekly prayer and support from a faithful friend, and my wife's unconditional love, I found my true identity. For the first time in my life, I began to see the false beliefs I had about myself, men, women and my sexuality, and my sexual orientation changed. God healed my mind and my heart, and then my behavior and sexual attractions changed. I now see other men as potential friends, not sexual partners.

The journey wasn't easy, but it was worth it. Today I am a whole person living authentically to who I am. My sexuality and behaviors are in line with my original design. For the last 18 years, I've been married to my beautiful wife, my gay porn addiction is gone, and now my sexual energy is directed toward her. I'm the happy, fulfilled father of a beautiful ten-year-old son and nine-year-old daughter.

"

Seminars helped put words and understanding to what I was experiencing. I no longer experience same-sex desires and have walked over 25 years in my choice.

GWEN GIBSON

Most of my life, including my childhood, I knew my attractions to women were not like those of my peers. I can't remember a time in my early life that wasn't filled with that thought. It wasn't until much later, after college, that I began to seriously consider coming out to friends and family. I confronted my own feelings and ventured into a same-sex relationship. I thought I'd be fulfilled, happy or at least relieved, but felt little more than momentary satisfaction. The emotional struggles, heavy drinking, depression and other relational disconnects in my life remained. Honestly, I was surprised. I thought a gay life was supposed to be my answer.

I had grown up in a Christian home and in the church. While I stopped going to church after college, I never lost the sense of loving God. It was the one relationship that felt more real to me than any other. I began an honest pursuit of God. It led me to books from others who had similar stories to mine, seminars that helped put words and understanding to what I was experiencing, and supportive prayer and spiritual counseling that helped me along the way. I was grateful for Christian pastors, who were accepting and gracious, and for both my straight and lesbian friends, who were genuinely supportive of my choice to live as a heterosexually-oriented woman.

I'm living an abundant life.

The change was steady, but not instant. I now no longer experience same-sex desires and have walked over 25 years in my choice. Much of my life has changed, including my emotional well-being and the lack of same-sex attraction. I'm living an abundant life as a single woman and have never considered living as I did before. I've been really happy with the choice I've made, even on the difficult days.

GWEN GIBSON

HARVEST ROCK CHURCH
harvestrock.church

DAVID KYLE FOSTER

"

The things that turned me on in men symbolized what I believed were absent in me.

DAVID KYLE FOSTER

Before I pursued change in my sexuality, I was deeply involved in the gay lifestyle while working as an actor in Hollywood. It was a lonely existence because the gay community was obsessed with youth and beauty. The shallowness of it all was very disheartening. Relationships lasted a very short time. Love was more sex and romance than commitment.

As a young man, I was hit on by older men daily, sometimes violently. The corruption of youth and the blind eye that everyone else turned was deeply troubling to me. Like so many gay men, I went through hundreds of partners trying to find someone who was capable of actually loving me, and it just wasn't there. We were all trying to fill a deep inner need that simply could not be found in gay relationships.

My homosexual drive stemmed from... a missing father figure.

Before it was all over, the emptiness and shallowness of it all had made me suicidal, alcoholic, drug addicted, venereally diseased, and very, very jaded. The so-called committed relationships were highly touted, but in reality were non-existent. In every case I knew of, I discovered both partners regularly cheating on their lovers, sometimes with me. There were no exceptions.

For all these reasons, I finally decided to pursue change. The last straw was the day I went to a gay club and saw all the lonely old men sitting at the bar drunk out of their minds while the younger people, many of whom were underaged, laughed and partied like there was no tomorrow. The old men drank themselves into a stupor every night because they were no longer young and beautiful. And as a result, no one wanted them. The only sex they got was when they paid young teens to go to bed with them.

I decided then and there I was not going to end up like that. At the same time, my substance abuse and sex addiction were out of control because I was using them to cope with the pain that came with my lifestyle. So I gave it all up and begged God to rescue me. I found my salvation through faith-based resources and pursuing a personal relationship with God. I discovered that my homosexual drive stemmed from a need to find a missing father figure.

The things that turned me on in men symbolized what I believed were absent in me. And I was also afraid of sexually mature women, which stemmed from several bad experiences with women during my youth.

After leaving the gay lifestyle and receiving healing for these underlying issues, my fear of women went away. My desire for a father figure was replaced with God being my father. As the brokenness was healed, my addictions simply went away because the pain that drove them was healed. And I finally was able to see myself complete as a man without trying to extract masculinity from other men.

As a result, my unhealthy coping mechanisms went away. The alcohol, the drugs, the sexual addiction and the suicidal thoughts all vanished. I've never been healthier in my life, and I would never go back to such a destructive life. In short, I was rescued from an early death and a very lonely, horrible life.

"

This ministry was my place of healing. They loved me every step of the way. This kind of love offered me hope, not just something to numb my pain.

CARMEN VAUGHT

Life before I pursued change felt out of control. It was a constant battle to find peace in who I was and to prove I was good.

When I started to have feelings for other girls, confusion entered in. I had no safe place to talk about it, and I believed the shame I carried would only grow if I admitted how I was feeling.

Because I was not like other girls and felt rejected by guys I liked, I felt unworthy in my femininity.

In my early 20s I began meeting people in the gay community, and I felt like I finally fit in. This community championed me to come out.

As I ran into the arms of this so-called love, my shame and self-hatred actually grew, and I felt that people in the Church and my family also hated me. I thought that if my family would just accept my sexuality, then I would be at peace and life would be amazing.

After 17 years of family heartache and separation, they started to express their love and admiration for me and to express their desire for relationship. I knew they didn't agree with my lifestyle, yet I felt their love for me. I thought I'd be ecstatic about that, but I actually found myself thinking, *Maybe I don't accept this life for myself.*

Six months later, my girlfriend of three years was cheating on me and moved out. I was miserable. The life I had pursued to find fulfillment left me at rock bottom instead. I was so scared to walk away from that identity because I didn't know who I was without it.

I finally told God, "I have no idea who I am, but You created me so You're going to have to tell me."

I decided to go back to church. On my first visit, I noticed an announcement for "a Christ-centered healing and support group for those seeking truth and grace in their sexuality and relationship with God." I attended the first meeting and when it was my turn to share why I was there, all I could say through my tears was "self-worth." This ministry was my place of healing. For the first time in my life, I felt like I could share my pain with others. We met for several months, uncovering the wounded places, and they loved me every step of the way, even in my mess. This kind of love offered me hope, not just something to numb my pain.

I love who I am. My life now has so much purpose.

As I looked to Jesus, my heart changed, and I began to understand who God created me to be. I accepted a relationship with Him, not a set of rules.

Now the internal battle is over, and I can walk in peace in my true identity. I love who I am and that I'm different than a lot of women.

My life now has so much purpose. I get to travel around the world and bring hope to others with my story of God's love. His plans are so much better than anything I ever imagined!

CARMEN VAUGHT

CHANGED MOVEMENT
changedmovement.com

APRIL LOCKHART

"

I watched personal testimonies on YouTube of many other ex-gays who talked about their journey. If they had found genuine transformation, then I could, too.

APRIL LOCKHART

My former life looked flashy and full of fun—lots of sex, alcohol and crazy partying. But I was just trying to distract myself from my own misery. I longed for stability and a relationship that would last. I felt like I was on an emotional roller coaster. There were times that felt good, but there were also a lot of lows. I experienced so much anxiety and depression that I began to believe those feelings were a part of me.

I was gay as far back as I can remember. I had no desire for male companionship because the opposite sex was repulsive to me. Just to make sure I was really gay, I dated two guys, and honestly, men were of no interest to me. Relationship with them felt forced and awkward.

Even when I found the girl of my dreams who was perfect in every way, I was so unhappy in that relationship. There was always something missing, but I could never figure out what it was. No matter what I did or had, I couldn't fill this longing. I was never happy or satisfied, and my depression and anxiety escalated to serious panic attacks.

I began planning my own suicide. I didn't want to break my mother's heart, so I planned it to look like an accident. I tried twice but failed both times.

Fast forward to today. My life is the polar opposite of what it was before. I'm 100% free of the emotional roller coaster and have no desire to engage in same-sex relations. I married an absolutely incredible man and have two boys and a girl. They are my constant reminders of how good God is to me and how he pulled me out. I don't suffer from depression or anxiety and I'm not on a constant search to fulfill an inner need. My once heavy heart now feels light. Some days I cry tears of joy because I still don't understand how someone like me could have all this.

It was the best choice I ever made.

Everything began to change for me when I decided I didn't want to be gay anymore although it was a process. I read books that encouraged me and joined a small group Bible study that let me be open, share my struggle, and have access to encouragement. I read my Bible constantly and implemented its principles in my life. I personally did not know of any other gay people like me that I could partner with, so I watched personal testimonies on YouTube of many other ex-gays who were coming out to talk about their journey. I found it extremely helpful to see how others had experienced change in their sexual desires. It was like a candle of hope held up for me when I grew weak. If they had found genuine transformation, then I could, too. I did. And it was the best choice I ever made.

MJ NIXON

RAINBOW REVIVAL
rainbowrevival.org

“

Community and accountability were key in my journey. I began to understand the truth of who I truly am.

MJ NIXON

Being born into a conservative Christian family, I was taught right from wrong at a young age, but I could never reconcile my faith with the attractions that lingered within. Being the middle child with two brothers, I started taking on their attributes and mentalities. This shaped my mindset from a healthy understanding of femininity to embracing a more masculinized identity. Outwardly, I was a rough and tumble tomboy, but inwardly, attractions towards females began to grow. Not knowing who to talk to or how to even share, I hid my attractions for my whole childhood and adolescence.

Now I live to share my story and tell others about the transformation I have experienced.

In college, everything changed. I was away from home and finally in an environment of acceptance. One day, a woman caught my eye; a friendship was formed, and a sexual relationship followed. Through this new relationship, I expressed my hidden inward attractions toward females for the first time in my life. We lived together for five years and envisioned a future together. Despite the deep bond this created, there was still a pull to end that relationship and seek after one with God. I really had always had an inner tug of war going on that caused me to question my attraction to her and my relationship with Jesus. Ultimately, I understood this inner conflict was directing me to the truth of my life as a woman.

The Bible was the greatest resource in my journey of freedom from homosexuality, along with videos of former LGBTQ members on YouTube and Vimeo. I attended a small group for people seeking healing from sexual brokenness, which was a huge support for me. Community and accountability were key in my journey. I began to understand the truth of who I truly am. Now I live to serve others, share my story and tell others about the transformation I have experienced. And I have seen God lead others into happy and free lives, healing their hearts the way He did mine.

"

Today I am fulfilled, joyful, and feminine—all things that I never was while living as a lesbian. I am no longer sexually attracted to women.

ELIZABETH WONING

Throughout most of my life I never belonged. I always felt excluded, and I questioned my sexuality and my gender. I hated the idea of being feminine because it was so foreign. I didn't feel like a girl, but I also didn't identify as a boy.

I made my first meaningful connection with another woman when I was in my mid-teens. We had such deep intimacy and love that our bond set a standard for my other relationships for several years. Though I occasionally dated men, and briefly in my early 20s was married to a man, I never developed fulfilling or lasting relationships with them.

I "came out" when I was in my early 20s after my brief marriage fell apart. I felt lesbianism explained my childhood and young adult experiences. I thought I was finally being authentic and true to myself. As a lesbian I felt powerful and asserted myself in stereotypically masculine ways. I adopted men's attire and a crewcut.

I am a strong advocate for their empowerment to overcome the effects of injustices against them.

During those years I found family and support as a lesbian living within the gay communities of large cities. I decided I wanted to attend seminary, and I did so as one of just a handful of openly gay students. After seminary I began working with youth, but questioned my faith.

In that season I re-evaluated what I believed about God, what I believed about the Bible, and what I believed about myself. Through that process I realized it was possible that some of my ideology had been wrong. I resolved to follow my faith sacrificially, which required reconsidering what I understood the Christian sexual ethic to be.

Up to that point, I believed I was born gay and that God had created me that way. As I further studied Christian doctrine, eventually I no longer believed I was born a lesbian. My experience of God's love, the Christian community around me, and my desire to pursue a life of prayer had a dramatic influence on my life.

I came to terms with the impact misogyny had on my self-perception and pursued pastoral care and counseling that addressed childhood hurts and perceptions. Above all, I acknowledged I had rejected myself as a woman.

I did not specifically seek change in my sexuality; nevertheless, I began experiencing changes in my sexual desires. I became attracted to a man, which was one of the most unexpected and humiliating experiences of my life, since I had so fully identified as a lesbian. He and I got married and have had a strong marriage since 2005. Today I am fulfilled, joyful, and feminine—all things that I never was while living as a lesbian. I am no longer sexually attracted to women. Rather, I am a strong advocate for their empowerment to overcome the effects of injustices against them.

ELIZABETH WONING

CHANGED MOVEMENT
Co-founder
changedmovement.com

STEPHEN BLACK

STEPHEN BLACK
Pastor, Author, Speaker
stephenblack.org

"

I began to pursue change through counseling and getting help with emotional healing. A year and a half later, I met my wife. We have now been married for 37 years.

STEPHEN BLACK

I was molested as a six-year-old, and again at age ten. I was bullied a lot and got beaten up. By the time I was in junior high, everyone was calling me *gay*, and I believed it. I was deeply depressed by eighth grade and had an older guy tell me he wanted to "show me the ropes" of the homosexual community.

For the next eight years, I lived in that community and had relationships with a number of very wealthy and powerful men. I was a boy toy.

I did have a couple of significant gay relationships, but by the end of them, I became very disillusioned. Then my little brother died, and his death caused me to re-evaluate my life and my beliefs. For a year and a half, I wrestled with what I believed, and then I gave my life to Jesus. I told God that if He would change me, I was willing to change.

I began to pursue change through counseling and getting help with emotional healing. A year and a half later, I met my wife. We have now been married for 38 years. We have three children and three grandchildren.

For the first ten years after I decided I wanted to change, my attraction to men was fading away. These last 15 years, I stopped experiencing same-sex attraction altogether.

“

“It is my hope to one day see a paradigm shift wherein medical science embraces the growing evidence that refutes the dangerous procedures and drugs endorsed by WPATH and wherein the so-called ‘transgender medical’ industry openly refutes procedures and drugs to identify as the opposite sex, calling them ineffective or harmful, as evidence supports.”

JEREMY BATE

STORIES OF DETRANSITION

Imagine not knowing whether you are a man or a woman.

Few topics encapsulate the confusion and pain of our generation as dramatically as gender identity. In this sensitive space, God meets us. His gentleness leads us to self-discovery, where we are reconciled to our bodies and can embrace the miracle of male and female as God has designed.

The stories in this section (bordered in blue) have never been more relevant and significant than they are right now. These men and women have walked out a journey that thousands are taking because of childhood gender transition procedures. They have desisted, or "detransitioned," after identifying as transgender.

We dedicate this section to all those today who find themselves questioning their own sex and gender, who wonder how God will respond when they trust Him.

KATHYGRACE DUNCAN

CHANGED MOVEMENT
changedmovement.com

KATHYGRACE IN HIGH SCHOOL

KATHYGRACE AS "KEITH"

TODAY

FORMERLY LIVED AS MALE

"

Because my dad was verbally and emotionally abusive to my mom, I believed that women were hated, vulnerable, and weak.

KATHYGRACE DUNCAN

From the time I was three years old, I felt and believed that I was born into the wrong body. What I saw in the mirror didn't match what I felt to be true. Life within a dysfunctional family only exacerbated my feelings. Because my dad was verbally and emotionally abusive to my mom, I believed that women were hated, vulnerable, and weak. When I was seven, my brother's entrance into the world was enthusiastically celebrated, cementing the lie that boys were more worthy of affirmation than girls. Then around the age of eight, I found an article about a woman living as a man; I felt excited to learn that this was possible! However, before I had the opportunity to even explore my options, I was molested by a family member. I was only 10 years old when the sexual abuse began, and it continued until I was 12. That painful experience further reinforced my feelings of weakness and vulnerability. Desperate to escape my circumstances and embrace my "true self," I finally moved out of the house when I was 19, changed my name, and began to take hormones to look like a man. Eventually, I had top surgery.

Today I am very content with who I am.

For the most part, I liked living life as a "transgender man." But I was also detached from my emotions. Determined to have a normal life, I worked really hard at maintaining my false identity. Things began to unravel a bit, however, when I broke up with a woman whom I had been dating for about five years. I quickly rebounded and jumped into another relationship, during which I developed a deep addiction to pornography. We had been together for only a year when I realized that I had become just as abusive and controlling as my dad, and the woman I was dating was as weak as my mom. Realizing it wouldn't work, I ended the relationship. What happened next would change my destiny.

Ironically, in the weeks after I had begun my efforts to live life like a man, I had attended a church and accepted Jesus as my Savior, only to be discovered and kicked out of that fellowship. Years later, I was attending a different church. I had gotten involved in the orchestra, and on my way to practice one evening, I actually heard God's audible voice questioning me: "Will you now? Will you now?" In that moment, I took an inventory of my life and saw nothing to hinder me. "Yes, Lord," I replied, "I will." Supernaturally, I was delivered from my addiction to pornography that night. Convinced of God's love for me, I earnestly sought the Lord for the next four years while still living as a man. Then, one day at church, I was confronted by one of the pastors. I confessed, "I am a woman living as a man." At that point of confession, I felt the wind of the Lord blow intensely into me. It was as if He was right in my face, blowing my hair back. I suddenly knew deep in my spirit I had to go back to being the woman He created me to be.

My journey back to the truth of who I was began that day. I was 30 years old. Instead of therapy or counseling, I began to explore my identity issues with the help of the Lord—via loving mentors He brought into my life, prayer and the Bible. As I began to discover who I was in God's eyes, change gradually began to take place. Working through issues of forgiveness has been a key part of my story. One of the hardest, most significant things I did during this process was to forgive my dad. The deep healing that I experienced as I confronted the painful memories and the hurtful words I had absorbed was worth it. Though my life was somewhat stable when I lived as a transgender man, I began to recognize how the lack of affirmation and love had led me to live in a constant state of fear and rejection.

It took five years for the effects of the hormones to wear off and for me to come to a place where I could begin to live as a woman again. Though fully restored on the inside, I still live with some of the impact of the hormones on my body. My voice remains slightly deeper, and I struggle with some hair loss. Fortunately, I did have breast reconstruction, and today I am very content with who I am. I understand that I am fiercely loved by Jesus. I can feel and express emotions unhindered by the fear of rejection. Sometimes I wonder whether my story would look different if someone in my life had just loved me, shown me that they wanted me, and had given me the truth without condemnation or judgment. That is why my heart's desire is to continue to bring hope to those who are hurting and desire change and why I also lead ministry within Portland Fellowship and CHANGED Movement. Above all else, I want to share truth. My hope is to work full-time with youth (or others) who identify as transgender and who long for a restored life.

"It took five years for the effects of the hormones to wear off and for me to come to a place where I could begin to live as a woman again."

TODAY

"

Though my life was somewhat stable when I lived as a man, I began to recognize how the lack of affirmation and love had led me to live in a constant state of fear and rejection.

KEVIN WHITT

KEVIN TODAY

kevinwhitt.org

"

My "gender identity" varied depending on the day. On some days I identified as "trans," on others as a woman, and very occasionally, I identified as a man.

KEVIN WHITT

I grew up in a dysfunctional home with a very abusive father. Born with a rare heart defect, I was a sickly child, and I was also very sensitive. As a result, my dad rejected me at an early age. He hated that I wasn't drawn to the same activities as most boys, so he abused me in an attempt to "teach me to be a man." The abuse was verbal, physical, and even sexual. "Men masturbate every day," he instructed me. In the first grade, everyone called me "gay" and "faggot" because I seemed more effeminate than other boys. My classmates would say, "Why do you walk like a girl? Why do you talk like a girl?" Words are powerful, and I believed the lie that I was inherently different from others. I had trouble fitting in. The bullying continued my entire life, from name-calling and gay bashing to all-out fights. At times it seemed like the entire school was against me. These early experiences taught me that men were evil. Women were, in fact, the only ones who had treated me like a real human, with love. So naturally, I rejected all things masculine.

Over the next years, I began having same-sex attraction at a young age, and at 15, I "came out" and started occasionally dressing in drag. Eventually, I adopted the persona of a woman full-time. Since I felt terribly inadequate at being a man, I decided I would be the most beautiful woman I could be. Perhaps if I reached "feminine perfection," I would finally feel normal.

I was embraced and accepted into a community of people with whom I could relate, and the attention and recognition of dressing in drag became addictive. In the '90s we didn't have the various pronouns that many prefer today, so I was limited as to how I could describe myself. But given the option, I would have identified more along the lines of non-binary because my "gender identity" varied depending on the day. On some days I identified as "trans," on others as a woman, and very occasionally, I identified as a man. I basically lived in a state of confusion over my sex my entire life.

When I was about 18, I went to therapy for the first time, where I was diagnosed with Borderline Personality Disorder connected to trauma I experienced as a child. Then, a few years later, I pursued counseling with a gender therapist who directed me to begin identifying as a woman. At that point, I had laser hair removal and took cross-sex hormones until I began experiencing the precursors of a stroke. About the same time, I got into the club scene as an entertainer. Desperate for money, I started working in the adult industry as a transsexual prostitute, phone sex operator, dominatrix, and webcam model. I thought this would be temporary, but earning over $1,000 a day became addictive, and I couldn't stop. Men made me feel sexy and desirable. (It's important to note that many trans-identifying people go into sex work because they often feel people are just going to use them for sex anyway. So why not charge for it? Often disowned by their families, many have low self-worth.)

For a while I was happy living as a woman. Because sex stereotypes were so ingrained in my mind, I didn't know it was possible for me to live life as a sensitive man. The idea that God had created me to be more sensitive and creative had never crossed my mind, so I lived my life as if I had been born in the wrong body. Eventually, however, I got tired of being a sexual fetish for men. What's more, I couldn't understand why none of those with whom I was romantically involved would commit to me. They would tell me all the right things, but I ultimately felt used. Over time I realized how toxic and addictive my lifestyle had become. Many friends and acquaintances had died young from HIV, suicide, and drug overdoses. Others were ruining their lives with drug and alcohol addictions.

One day while I was working in a gay male strip club, one of the stripper boys invited me to go to church. I thought it was weird, but I was open to it, and I went. Honestly, I hated Christians because all I felt I'd ever been taught by the church was that "gay people were going to hell," and their punishment from God was to contract AIDS and die. So, I figured, if I'm going to hell, I might as well have fun doing it. But the day I attended church with my friend, a seed was planted in my heart. A few months later, I got invited to church on Easter Sunday. God grabbed my attention through a modern-day version of the resurrection of Christ being played out on stage, and I began to cry. I saw all that Jesus had done for me. That was the first day of my journey away from transgender identity.

Within months, my desire to do drag, party, or have sex lessened. At 35 years old, I began to hear God speaking quietly to my heart about avoiding temptation. After much prayer and a desire to obey Him, I knew I needed to get rid of all of my women's clothing and accessories. My heart began to change dramatically as God continued to show me my true identity. I did not come to Christ seeking changes to my gender or sexual identity. Simply desiring a healthy life, I kept an open mind and a loving heart. He did the rest. Fortunately, my consumption of hormones was so short-lived that the impact on my body was minimal. Though I still have some chest sensitivity, today, my body is whole. My mental health is also much improved, although I do still have some mental health issues from the trauma and abuse I endured throughout my life.

"

I did not come to Christ seeking changes to my gender or sexual identity. Simply desiring a healthy life, I kept an open mind and a loving heart. He did the rest.

I now understand that my sensitivity and interests in art, fashion, and beauty do not mean that I am the wrong sex or homosexual. I wish I had been offered therapy to get to the roots of why I had those feelings of gender dysphoria. Sadly, American culture places a stigma on men. Common messaging today is that if we don't watch football and act a

KEVIN AS A TRANSSEXUAL PROSTITUTE

certain way, we must be gay or in the wrong body. But that is a lie. I am created in God's image, and He gave me a creative mind. Today, I love being the man I was designed to be. I am able to be myself without hiding behind a costume to feel worthy. I no longer need to pretend to be something I'm not. It's very freeing to love who God created me to be. I have different desires now—different interests and hobbies. I finally realized there is more to life than clubs, makeup and dresses, sex, men, and alcohol. God changed everything about me, and I recognize my great value and worth.

My hope is to continue fighting for children so they don't have to go through what I went through in the quest for identity. Ultimately, I'd like to get married one day and have children.

RUTH SHEKINAH NOEL

RUTH AS RAJ

RUTH TODAY

KINGDOMCITY
Young Adult Group Leader
kingdomcity.com

“

Not only did my cheating girlfriend break up with me for attending a church, but the “trans woman” (my now-husband Simon) and I were both thrown out of the church.

RUTH SHEKINAH NOEL

WIFE TO SIMON / PAGE 70

I grew up in a strict Punjabi family in Malaysia. A tomboy at heart, I always loved sports, and because I wasn't allowed to cut my hair, I would stuff it under a ball cap. Other than the fact that I was secretly molested by a neighbor and a cousin as a child, life was relatively normal until I was 16 years old. That's when I attended my aunt's wedding in India for a month. Though I had a boyfriend back home, I became attracted to a distant female cousin, and I couldn't get her out of my mind. Feeling drawn to her, I began to act more stereotypically masculine. I felt like a boy, and she treated me like one, too. This was the first time I realized I had gender dysphoria and same-sex attraction.

My entire family—all of my relatives—decided to disown me.

Once home, I became curious to know whether other girls experienced similar feelings. I turned to Google and YouTube for answers and learned I was not alone. In fact, I learned I wasn't a girl at all. Because I was having these feelings, the internet taught me I must have been born in the wrong body. As I continued to watch “trans men” on YouTube, I was excited about how good they looked, and I was encouraged to come out as the person I thought I was meant to be. *This isn't a disease*, I thought. *This is normal.* Because I knew my family wouldn't approve, I lived secretly this way until I was 25, stuffing my long hair under my cap and binding my chest. But when I turned 25, my parents began to talk to me about marriage. Having already spurned guys “because they only wanted sex,” I knew I needed to come out to my parents, or my life would be ruined. Though my father was disappointed, he really didn't say much. But when I cut my hair, my mom became furious and started hitting me. She even brought a knife to kill me. What's more, my entire family—all of my relatives—decided to disown me. Undeterred, I continued to alter my appearance by packing my pants and applying ointment to my face to grow a beard. I avoided hormones because I didn't want to deal with the side effects. Though I initially wanted to take testosterone, the procedure seemed too complicated, and I was afraid of injections. I couldn't afford a mastectomy, so like other trans men I'd seen, I worked out really hard to naturally reduce the size of my breasts. Within a month, I had a beard, and no one knew I was a woman. People started addressing me as "sir," and women started noticing me and calling me handsome. I was loving my life and feeling more confident about myself. The only problem was that girls kept coming in and out of my life. For the next few years, I experienced a revolving door of heartbreak. Though I had assumed I would be able to fulfill a woman's need for love better than sex-obsessed men, my relationships never lasted. What's worse, some of the women were bad influences, and I began to drink and smoke. Eventually, I lost everything I had—house, car, bike, work, and money. I was laden with debt and hounded by loan sharks.

The next day, he cut his hair, and I shaved my beard, plucked my eyebrows, and removed the binder from my chest.

Miraculously, one of my friends introduced me to Jesus, and when I stepped into a church for the first time, I felt an incredible peace. I shared my story with the pastor and told him I wanted to marry my current girlfriend. When he said I wasn't meant to be a man, I refused to listen. In an effort to convince me to change, he introduced me to a "transgender" woman attending his church who was unhappy with the decisions she had made and the surgeries she had endured. He wanted to make sure that I understood the consequences of my lifestyle. The moment we met each other, however, we fell in love! It was truly love at first sight! Not only did my cheating girlfriend break up with me for attending a church, but this "trans woman" (my now-husband Simon) and I were both thrown out of the church. That's when we found Kingdomcity, the church we attend today.

Still embracing our transgender identities, we began dating. During a sermon series on healthy relationships, the pastor began to teach from Genesis about God's design for marriage and His creation of man and woman. I instantly fell under the conviction of the Holy Spirit. Immediately, my heart began racing. I knew at that moment that the answer to my problems was rooted in my identity. *I am created as female*, I said to myself, *but I want to be a male*, which is against the law of creation. With this revelation, I prayed in my heart, "Lord, I am willing to change; please change her (Simon), too, as I love her so much it does not matter if she is a female or a male. I want to marry her." Miraculously, Simon decided he, too, would desist. The next day, he cut his hair, and I shaved my beard, plucked my eyebrows, and removed the binder from my chest.

Physically, it only took me a day to revert back to female. (I still grow facial hair, and I have to go for threading every week.) But, it took at least a year for me to adjust emotionally to the change. Today, happily married to Simon, I am still learning to fully embrace my femininity and am continuously asking God to teach me and mold me into the woman He wants me to be. My friends, family, and coworkers are surprised at how feminine and beautiful I have become. The Lord has guided me through each and every step, as I never liked to dress up, wear makeup, or even walk like a lady. By His grace, everything is changing, and others are noticing the differences in me. Now, instead of searching YouTube for "how-to-transition" videos, I watch sermons on women's empowerment, which have helped me in this journey. There are many resources on how to become "transgender," but very few that explain how to avoid this sin and trap. If I had received counseling or if I had been able to find videos explaining how to overcome gender dysphoria, my story may have been different.

Today, I know I am a child of God, created in His image to be a woman, and when I struggle, I can count on Him to lead me. My hope for the future is to be used by God mightily. Now that He has saved me, I would like to spread this good news to others so that they, too, can experience His love.

RUTH TODAY WITH HUSBAND, SIMON

"

Though I had assumed I would be able to fulfill a woman's need for love better than sex-obsessed men, my relationships never lasted.

SIMON NOEL

SIMON NOEL NOW

SIMON AS SANJANA

KINGDOMCITY
Young Adult Group Leader
kingdomcity.com

"

In the early days of our relationship, Ruth (who is now my wife) and I were both still embracing our transgender identities.

SIMON NOEL

HUSBAND TO RUTH / PAGE 66

I identified as a "transgender woman" in Malaysia for 18 years. I began to feel like I was a girl at a young age as a result of frequent sexual abuse, which began when I was nine years old. I was molested secretly by trusted adults, but I was too afraid to tell my family. As a result of the abuse, I became uncomfortable around men, assuming they were all sexual predators. I felt safer with my mother and my aunts and began to identify more closely with them. When I looked in the mirror, I always saw myself as a girl, and as a result, I began to develop a feminine-like shyness, as well as girlish mannerisms. As I developed same-sex attraction, I wanted men to notice me more. My parents, however, did not approve of my effeminate behavior, so I was frequently scolded and beaten and was often the subject of their arguments.

Ever since I surrendered to the Lord, He has walked with me through every phase of reclaiming my true identity.

Then, when I was 13, my male cousin, who had already begun identifying as a woman, took me to a brothel to meet the oldest trans-identifying person in Malaysia. The place was filled with "transgender women," who, to me, looked very beautiful. Because I had been experiencing dysphoria as well as same-sex attraction, I was drawn to their lifestyle. *This is who I'm meant to be,* I thought to myself. After returning home, I started to steal my mother's makeup. I also fantasized about piercing my nose and ears to wear long earrings.

Within a year, I ran away to visit the brothel again and to further explore the idea of trying to identify as a woman. As I watched and listened to these "trans women," I became even more interested in adopting their lifestyle. They coached me on how to make changes and even suggested surgeries to help me manifest feminine-like features. Honestly, it was an exciting journey for me, as I was able to embrace a feminized identity without fear. One transgender friend in particular became my mentor. In retrospect, I believe she actually brainwashed me

> "
>
> God has assured me that despite the physical damage done to my body, I am still a man, and He loves me just the same.

to go through with surgeries. Unfortunately, I did not know enough to question her advice. There was no education about masculinity offered anywhere and no understanding counselors who could help me make sense of my feelings. If I had been given the motivation to build my life and carry on as a man, I would likely have chosen a different path.

Without proper guidance, however, at age 20 I started consuming hormone pills and performing laser hair removal on my face. At first, the pills made me feel sick, so I tried injections instead. As my skin started getting tighter and softer, I told myself, "The man is gone, and the woman is here." After that, I started waxing my legs and growing out my hair. Because I needed money to buy more girly stuff, I began working in a nightclub as a dancer. I knew that the curvier I looked, the more money I would make, so I decided to have breast augmentation and silicone injections in my hips. I felt victorious once the surgery was completed! It was an amazing feeling to look at myself and seem to see a "real" woman. However, after two years, I started feeling dissatisfied with my lower body. I told myself it was not enough to have breasts, but I also needed to have a vagina if I truly wanted to please a man. So, I went through with my bottom operation. Although the surgery was extremely painful, I felt it would be worth it in the end. By age 25, I was "fully transitioned," and though I was satisfied with my looks, my lower body remained numb for almost two years.

At first, I felt very happy with my new life. People praised my beauty everywhere I went, and I felt like I was living a dream. Many men pursued me, and I was often the center of attention. To further solidify my new identity, I got a doctor's letter confirming that I was a woman despite the male name on my identity card. I had a job as well as a bunch of girlfriends; no one knew I was actually a man unless I told them. Life was amazing.

During this time, I had one long-term relationship that lasted for five years. I loved this man from the bottom of my heart, but I felt used by him for sex and money. Eventually, he took all my money and left me. I was so brokenhearted that I wanted to end my life, and in fact, I attempted suicide by hanging myself from the ceiling fan. At that moment, I literally felt my spirit leave my body and float above me, but the very next second, I rapidly dropped back onto earth and was revived as the ceiling broke down. Somehow, I knew that God was giving me a second chance.

After this incident, my mother started meeting with me and speaking with me about God. Before, I would get irritated whenever she mentioned Jesus because I had been worshiping idols even though I was born into a Christian home. But this time was different. Something inside of me was ready to listen. Simultaneously, the trans-identifying friend who persuaded me to have surgery insisted that I go to Indonesia as a prostitute, but this time, I refused.

At a loss for what to do, I called my mother and asked if she would accept me back; I was 28 years old when I moved home. My mother then invited me to church with her, and slowly I started pursuing the Lord. I left all of my bad habits behind, like drinking, smoking, drugs, and pubs. But I was still living and dressing as a woman. Then, one day my pastor, who knew I was trying to straighten out my life, asked me if I would counsel a "trans man" who was considering surgery. I wasn't really ready to engage or counsel others since I still looked like a woman, but because the pastor had asked me to, I agreed. I was shocked as this "man" entered the room. It was love at first sight, and I had to tell the pastor I couldn't counsel this "man." It was too much for me. Smitten with one another, we were both thrown out of the church when we began a relationship. That is when we found Kingdomcity, the church we still attend today.

In the early days of our relationship, Ruth (who is now my wife) and I were both still embracing our transgender identities. Then, one Sunday our pastor preached about healthy relationships. As he talked about God's design for marriage and His creation of male and female, we both fell under the conviction of the Holy Spirit. Immediately, I sensed that the life I was living was not right. Ruth felt exactly the same! At that moment, we both knew we needed to repent. Once back home, I decided to cut my hair and desist back to male. My family, who had been praying for me for years, greatly rejoiced. Miraculously, the moment I determined to desist, my beard and mustache started growing again. Within two months, I underwent surgery for the removal of my breast implants. To my surprise, the same doctor who performed my initial augmentation was now helping me to desist. Remembering me, he apologized for doing my augmentation in the first place. A year after desisting, Ruth and I were married, and today, we lead a ministry group at our church.

It has been six years since I stopped identifying as a woman, and ever since I surrendered to the Lord, He has walked with me through every phase of reclaiming my true identity. In my brokenness, I had been seeking a worldly love that I thought would satisfy. But after the Lord set me free, I experienced a greater love. Sometimes, I cannot believe that I am actually living as a man and doing those things that men do. Even so, I still battle the side effects of the surgeries and cross-sex hormones I subjected myself to. The silicone damaged the nerves in my thighs, making it difficult to walk long distances or perform strenuous activities, and weight gain in the absence of hormone supplements is an issue. Desisting has been something of a battle, especially since I cannot reverse my bottom surgery. And despite removing my implants, I still have a bumpy chest, so I sometimes struggle with dysphoria because I don't exactly look like a normal man. Nonetheless, God has assured me that despite the physical damage done to my body, I am still a man, and He loves me just the same. I know He will continue to mold me to become the man He created me to be. It helps when I remember that it's the condition of my heart, and not my body, that is of utmost importance to God.

SIMON NOW WITH HIS WIFE, RUTH

MICHAEL EDWARD UKUS

MICHAEL AS A LADYBOY

MICHAEL TODAY

"

There was a figure wearing white clothing... He looked me straight in the eyes and said, "Don't be afraid; trust Me. No one will be harmed."

MICHAEL EDWARD UKUS

I grew up in a Christian home in Manado, Indonesia. The second of three children, I lived a fairly normal life until I was about 19 years old. After I enrolled in a Christian university to study theology, my parents unexpectedly divorced, and my dad abandoned our family. As my world was crumbling around me, I began to question my faith. After getting drunk one night on Cap Tikus, a typical Mandonese booze, I was gang raped by a group of 13 senior students at my school. The abuse continued beyond that night—for about a year and a half. Though I was initially scared and confused by my feelings, eventually, I began to enjoy gay sex. That's when I decided to fully embrace gay culture and sexuality. Soon I became addicted to drugs and sex, to the point that I began to pimp young girls and also prostitute myself as a "ladyboy" just to support my hedonistic habits. Even though my counselor warned me that I was headed down a dangerous path, I ignored his advice, and my life spiraled downward. In all, I lived life as a "transgender woman" for about seven years. At one point, I considered surgical procedures and pharmaceuticals, but I could never seem to save enough money to go through with any treatments or surgeries. As fast as I made it, I would spend it on drugs and sex. But it didn't matter. My hair grew long, and my body became tiny, and everyone thought I really was a girl.

Every sin I'd ever committed was flashing before my eyes as if I was watching a movie of my life.

During those years, I felt free and I didn't really care about the opinions of others. I felt respect from many people who didn't judge me and just accepted me for who I was. But despite the affirmation I received from many friends, I felt empty on the inside. Honestly, my life had become so gripped by sin that I thought it was too late to come back to God. My family had quit advising me, and I believed no one could help me. So I rebelled even further. *Might as well go all the way to the bottom*, I thought. At one point, I overdosed on drugs, and my lungs were in horrible condition. The doctor said that I might not live more than a month, but through prayer I was healed. You would think that brush with death would have been my wake-up call, but after recovery, I fell again to my old vices: drugs, clubs, and sex. That's when God intervened.

I was on a boat from Manado to Tahuna with my mom and

my stepfather in late 2009. Suddenly, in the middle of the sea, a ferocious storm arose. We were being tossed by strong waves and wind. I remember it was 9 p.m. when all of a sudden, the boat lunged to the left and then to the right, bursting open the doors on the second deck. Gripped with fear, people were screaming and crying. This continued for at least eight hours. Half of the passengers' belongings were thrown into the sea, and the light on the boat began to dim. Donning life jackets, we were prepared to jump at the crew's orders. It was that bad. Many of the passengers were singing worship songs over and over. But the only thing I could think about was my sins. It was as if every sin I'd ever committed was flashing before my eyes as if I was watching a movie of my life. But then I felt something in my heart encourage me to pray. "Lord," I said, "I know I have sinned, but I don't want to see my mom suffer because of me. I beg you, Lord, even if I have to die, let my mom live. However, if you are willing, I beg you to save us from this trial, and I promise you I will return, repent, and serve you all of my life." When I opened my eyes, I could see clearly at the end of the boat there was a figure wearing white clothing walking around the edge of the boat with one hand touching the edge and the other hand on the wall of the boat. He looked me straight in the eyes and said, "Don't be afraid; trust Me. No one will be harmed."

That incident brought me back to God. He changed my life, restored me, and gave me hope for the future. Because I'd never had any surgical procedures, I was able to begin living as a man immediately. I cut my hair and threw out my women's clothing soon after I was saved. Emotionally, however, the journey took a little longer. My friends slowly drifted away from me, and though this made me sad, I understood that the decision to live a new life would be accompanied by struggles. I received counseling from my pastor and much prayer and support from my family and church friends. This helped me cut ties with my past and dare to move on. Today, more than 10 years later, I'm still free. As I continue embracing my identity as a man, I'm still healing. Single and serving in a local church in Jakarta, Indonesia, I depend on the Lord daily for my wholeness and freedom. I hope that many people who are sexually confused will, like me, experience the power of God to bring healing to their lives and restore their identities.

"Despite the affirmation I received from many friends, I felt empty on the inside."

MICHAEL TODAY

“

Because I’d never had any surgical procedures, I was able to begin living as a man immediately. I cut my hair and threw out my women’s clothing soon after I was saved.

LAURA SMALTS

LAURA WITH HER HUSBAND TODAY

EDEN'S REDEMPTION
edensredemption.org

FORMERLY LIVED AS MALE

"

I had deep, bitter resentment against my mother that had gone unresolved for years, and as a result, I rejected all that she represented.

LAURA SMALTS

I developed feelings of confusion about my sex early in childhood. Raised in a Christian home, I had a strained relationship with my mom, who exhausted herself trying to be the perfect Christian. Frequently agitated and irritable, she often didn't want me around because I was hyper. To reinforce the sting, I learned she had miscarried two boys before having me. "You likely wouldn't be here if either of them had lived," she told me one day. Though her words were not meant to hurt me, I, naturally, felt guilty and rejected, which fed a deep inner turmoil about my identity as a girl. When I was molested at the age of eight, my behavior became very sexualized.

God began to reveal the unattractiveness and the irrationality of a "transgender" identity.

I spent the next 25 years trying to get fulfillment and love through sex. Feeling objectified by men in high school, I began to believe being female was disgusting, filthy, and worthless. I was sure I should have been a man, so I began the journey of "transitioning" to transform my appearance.

In 2007, at the age of 25, I started living full-time as Jake, and I thought I was on the road to freedom. If only I could have seen the hell that lay ahead. Before undergoing any surgeries or receiving drugs to alter my physical appearance, I was required to attend at least three one-hour counseling sessions with a licensed therapist. I had no interest in counseling. *Anyone who needs counseling is crazy*, I thought. I only went because it was required. During the third session, the therapist put down her notebook, looked right into my eyes, and said, "Wow, you really have issues with your mom." I was stunned! How did we get from talking about how I was really a man to talking about my mother? I blew up and spat back, "I am not here to talk about my mom!" She looked at me sadly and said softly, "So, you just want me to give you the letter?" (The letter would state I had been diagnosed with Gender Identity Disorder to authorize me to begin hormones. The letter would also give me access to locker rooms and bathrooms, if needed.) "Yes!" I snapped back. "That's all I'm here for. I don't need therapy!"

Looking back, I think she knew the truth: I had deep, bitter resentment against my mother that had gone unresolved for years, and as a result, I rejected all that she represented, including femininity. If I had allowed the therapist to help me work through those issues, I don't think I would have ever

BEFORE TRANSITION

LAURA LIVING AS JAKE

gone down the transgender road. Sadly, at the time, I was already convinced I was a man trapped in a woman's body and not willing to listen to another opinion. So I took my letter and ran.

I first began taking testosterone by injection. My voice began to deepen, I had more energy, I had an increased sex drive, and I was less emotional. Soon, I began to see my body composition change as my body and face began to look more masculine. (Later, the hormones began to make my face look puffy. This is a side-effect that happens in many female-to-male "gender transition" procedures. The hormones cause extraordinary weight gain and can make the face look swollen.) Eventually, I began to grow a beard, had a double mastectomy/chest reconstruction, had all my female procreative organs removed, and had all of the legal name- and gender- status changes so I could pass exclusively as a man.

After years of hormones and surgeries, I was empty and broken. I was devastated to realize that none of the changes I was making had actually made me a man, and I knew they never would. All I had done was change the outside. The result? I felt trapped in a world between male and female. I had often described myself before "coming out" as wearing a mask of a female identity. But within three years, my transgender identity had become the mask. What had promised to be freedom had, in fact, become my prison cell. I soon became enslaved to wearing clothes that never quite fit, injecting myself over and over with needles (hormones), and wearing prosthetics (a constant reminder of how fake it all was).

As the years passed, God gently drew me back toward Him. Though my relationship with my parents had been almost non-existent for years, aside from an occasional phone call or dinner meeting, my mom hired me to make a website for the Bible study she was teaching. Though I had no interest in Bible study, I agreed because I needed both the money and the experience. Little did I know God would use this project to crumble the defensive walls of pride that had kept Him on the outside for so long. As I read the words in the lessons, the ice that encased my heart began to melt. For the first time in my life, I began to see God's love and faithfulness in His Word.

Over the next few months, I began to call my mom every day after work. She patiently answered my questions about the Bible. One day, I said, "Mom, how did I get here? Six months ago, I was 180 degrees from where I am now. All I want is to hear the Word of God." She said, "I have been praying that God would draw you back like a magnet." And that's exactly what He had done! What's more, I realized that the angry, stressed-out, exhausted, legalistic mother I grew up with had been completely transformed, and her religion had been exchanged for real faith. The moment I recognized the dramatic changes in my mom was the moment I knew that the gospel was true. As a result, I wholeheartedly gave my life to Christ.

For the months that followed, I wrestled with God. I wanted so desperately to be a godly man. And I tried convincing myself that God had intended me to be a man. Then I heard Dr. Everett Piper on the radio say, "We are not just made up of our feelings, instincts, and inclinations. But we are made in the image of God, and we can choose our behavior, despite how we feel." As I began to wrestle with his words and admit that my circumstances were a choice, God began to reveal the unattractiveness and the irrationality of a "transgender" identity. One night, He asked me, "If you stood before me tonight, what name would I call?" That question stopped me in my tracks. I had hoped so desperately that God accepted me as Jake. But then, in the most loving voice I have ever heard, the Creator of the Universe whispered to me, "Let Me tell you who you are."

If I had allowed her to help me work through those issues, I don't think I would have ever gone down the transgender road.

Hit hard with conviction, I became desperate to escape this false identity and all that went with it, but I was afraid it was too late. I had lived in complete stealth, as I called it: no one except family and my partner knew I was a woman. I didn't know how to fix it. Over the next month, I struggled and cried out to God.

Then, one night I had a clear vision of Jesus getting down on one knee, reaching into the pit with arm outstretched toward me. He asked, "Do you trust me?" I knew He was asking me to leave everything and follow Him in faith. In turn, I walked away from everything I had known to follow Christ: my job, my partner of almost eight years, my financial security, and my entire identity. As difficult as it was, God cut the cord on my old life in miraculous ways. When I began to attend my mom's Bible study, I was met with overwhelming love from women I did not even know; they affirmed me and loved me as a woman, completely transforming my heart. The belief that I was meant to be a man, in fact, vanished. Immediately, I began to wear feminine clothing as God continued to peel away the layers of the proverbial onion to restore my identity. People who've known me are often shocked at how feminine I have become, and it's no act. I have simply allowed God to peel off the false masculinity in which I had covered myself.

Today, completely reconciled to my family, I continue to experience God's healing and restoration. In May of 2021, He brought an incredible man, Perry Smalts, into my life, and we married a year later in 2022. Perry is a husband beyond my wildest dreams. I had always believed the lie that I was not good enough to be a wife, that I was too emotional, and that I was "damaged goods." I wondered, *What man could ever accept not only my past as a "trans man" but also my sexual past?* Perry, a bi-vocational music minister and associate pastor who also works in insurance, has not only accepted and loved me but also says he doesn't see me as someone who once identified as transgender. He sees me as the new creature God created me to be when Christ came into my life, as stated in 2 Corinthians 5:17. God has used Perry not only to love me but also to teach me about Christ's love for His bride.

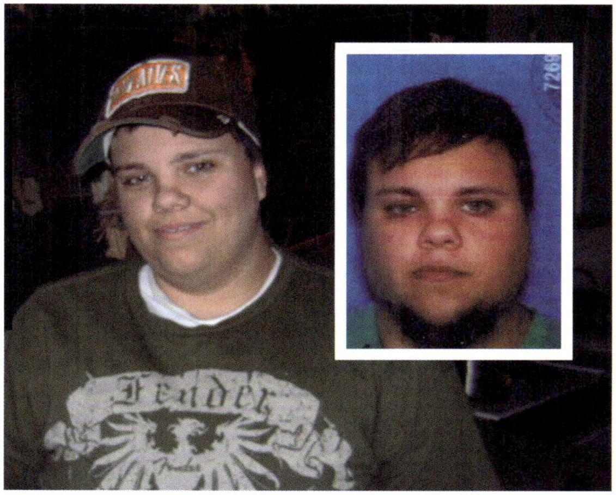

LAURA LIVING AS JAKE

JESUS CARBONELL

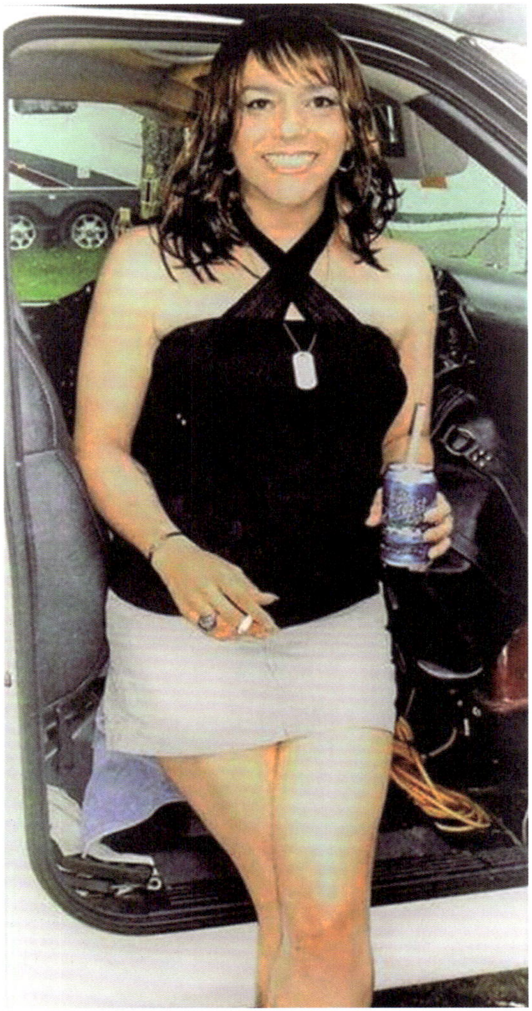

JESUS AS A TRANSGENDER WOMAN

JESUS TODAY

TRANSFORMED BY JESUS CHRIST

www.rutaeste.com/ruta-11

“

Honestly, I didn’t want to be a “trans woman”; I wanted to be a real woman.

JESUS CARBONELL

Born in Colombia, I grew up in a dysfunctional family where emotional violence and physical aggression were normal. My home environment, devoid of values and limits, was an extremely dangerous place for a child. I was six years old when I was first sexually molested, and abusive encounters with men (who were close to the family) continued for years.

In the absence of meaningful relationships, I never experienced the unconditional love I needed as a child. As I grew older, I began, without understanding, to mentally distort and sexualize my affections. I embraced a homosexual lifestyle at the age of 17, and because I'd always wanted to be like my sister and my aunts, I eventually took a turn toward “transgenderism,” occasionally dressing as a woman.

Because I'd always wanted to be like my sister and my aunts, I eventually took a turn toward “transgenderism.”

Life continued like this until I was in my late 30s. That's when I met a transgender woman—a man who identified as a woman. We spent a great deal of time together, and within months, I, too, began identifying as a woman. Like many friends, I began attending support groups that helped people psychologically prepare for feminizing surgeries. Shortly thereafter, I underwent mesotherapy injections (to shrink my waist and body fat), and had a facelift and received butt implants. At first, I was happy with the changes, but my new identity did not fit my concept of a woman. Honestly, I didn't want to be a “trans woman”; I wanted to be a real woman. I began to experience cycles of depression so severe that I often wished I was dead. My days were purposeless, and I struggled to find true inner fulfillment. My same-sex relationships only gave me fleeting moments of pleasure, and, honestly, they felt empty. I had hoped the “gender transition” would bring the fulfillment I'd longed for, but ultimately, I realized all my efforts had been in vain. To make matters worse, my butt implants became encapsulated, and I fell deathly ill with Hepatitis C and cirrhosis of the liver as a result of years of unbridled alcohol and drug use. When the doctors informed me there was nothing they could do to help me, I became bitter and very angry with God. I had asked Him countless times to remove my same-sex attraction; however, my prayers had not been answered. At least not yet.

I was literally on my deathbed in 2010, seemingly without hope, when the light of the Lord began to penetrate my world. Change began when my mother and my sister came to see me. My mother wanted to attend church, so I contacted a friend who had been inviting me to visit her church for three years. Although I was terribly sick, I decided to go along. My body was so swollen from liver failure that I could not even sit down during the service. Noticing my condition, several of the church members encouraged me to go to the altar for prayer. As they anointed me with oil and prayed for me, my healing began, not only physically but emotionally, mentally, and spiritually as well. After this experience, I began to meet with many Christians from the church. They embraced me and loved me unconditionally, and gradually my body and my spirit began to heal. I also began to identify once again as a man. Six months later, I got baptized in the name of Jesus. Almost immediately, I began to look and feel like the real person God created me to be. I knew Jesus had given me a new life and had made me whole in His love. I began to experience a confidence that I had never felt before. My transformation was radical; His power literally lifted me from my deathbed, healed me, and restored me from all my wounds. Today, 13 years later, I am living free and restored, and I'm hopeful for the future. In fact, I'd like to marry and have children.

Had someone offered me caring and unconditional support when I was a young person, along with God's biblical truths concerning sexuality, my story may have been different. That's why today I lead the ministry, Transformed by Jesus Christ, which offers loving and unconditional support to those in pain over same-sex attraction and educates family members, friends, pastors, and the church at large. We offer a program that raises awareness through education of emotions and spiritual freedom, edifying Christians to walk in freedom from sexual trauma and addictions through the power of the Holy Spirit. We also help family members who call for guidance.

"

I was literally on my death-bed in 2010, seemingly without hope, when the light of the Lord began to penetrate my world.

"His power literally lifted me from my deathbed, healed me, and restored me from all my wounds."

JESUS AS A TRANSGENDER WOMAN

JESUS TODAY

JEREMY BATE

JEREMY TODAY

“

I no longer suffer from debilitating depression, thanks to my awakening to a new life in Christ.

JEREMY BATE

Born in England in 1965, I first experienced conflict with my identity and questioned whether I was possibly a girl around age five. As I was learning to read, I realized I identified with the female characters in books, so I assumed I was supposed to be a girl. Ashamed, I kept these feelings hidden for most of my life, squashing and ignoring them as much as possible. Like an addict who can't get free, however, I could never seem to shake off the feeling that I had been born into the wrong body. When I was eight, my family moved to Australia, and by the time I was 16, we had stopped going to church. Although I had taken Catholicism seriously at times during my early life, I drifted away from the faith and became a pagan in my early 20s. I was indoctrinated to believe the lie that the church was hateful and bigoted, especially in regard to sexuality. During those years, I began a relationship with a woman, and we had two children, but eventually, the relationship broke down. When I was 30, I actually read the definition of transsexual for the first time and thought to myself, *this must be me!* Those feelings were confirmed by a psychologist whom I began seeing after my relationship split. When I said I was concerned about going against nature, she replied, “What about going against your own nature?”

I visited one psychologist and two psychiatrists, and none tried to find the root cause of my confusion.

From that point on, the predominant message that I came across from both media and books was very supportive of the trans phenomenon, convincing me that I was born this way and that the only solution was to embrace a new identity as a woman. Not much dissenting information existed at the time, but what I did find, I had already learned to frame as transphobic. In fact, I visited one psychologist and two psychiatrists, and none tried to find the root cause of my confusion about my sex. Because his previous trans-identifying patients had committed suicide, my first psychiatrist was reluctant to put me on cross-sex hormones. However, the second psychiatrist prescribed hormones straight away. Confident this was the right course of action, I continued to push forward with laser facial hair removal. By the time I was in my mid-30s, I had begun a relationship with a woman, who was very understanding. With her support, at age 38 I underwent a full suite of surgeries and procedures to look like a woman.

In total, I lived as if I were a woman for 20 years, and though I often felt awkward, I lived a fairly normal life. I even played women's soccer. But after my second relationship ended in 2010, I became very depressed and began to do a lot of soul searching. Though I didn't question that identity, it gradually began to feel less important to me. Seven years later, I had an awakening in which I began to question my politics as well as mainstream science. I realized much of what I had accepted as reality was not founded on objective truth. Science, I discovered, can be based on false assumptions and sometimes serves a political and ideological purpose. Nonetheless, I avoided questioning transgender science because I knew that it would likely lead to reversing all the efforts I had made to become a woman. Eventually, however, I had to face the facts. When I investigated, I found transgender science to be weak, flawed, biased, and lacking adequate peer review. That's when my journey toward desistance began in earnest. A YouTube lecture by a reputable doctor outlined how trans groups were lobbying within medical professional bodies to further the trans agenda by dictating a medical policy of "affirming" treatment. But what further sealed the deal was when I learned that my mother had taken DES (diethylstilbestrol), a potent estrogen and so-called anti-miscarriage drug prescribed to millions of women between the 1940s and 1970s. Research revealed that 20 percent of boys exposed to the drug in utero experienced dysphoria relating to their sex. I realized DES was likely the cause of that confusion. All of these revelations prompted me to desist and embrace my natal sex. I discussed my feelings about this with a "transhealth" social media group and was immediately banned for merely questioning the science.

I began taking testosterone at age 52, and within a few weeks, my male sex characteristics began to reemerge. Because of my surgeries, however, I knew I could never fully reverse the effects those procedures had on my body. I still have some breast growth that cannot be reversed. And, along with loss of fertility, I'm unable to produce my own hormones, which often results in migraines, hot flashes, and lethargy (during times of hormonal deficits). What's more, my pituitary gland is wildly hyperactive because it continues to try to get my non-existent testes to produce testosterone.

> "
>
> When I investigated, I found transgender science to be weak, flawed, biased, and lacking adequate peer review.

My journey to wholeness did not end with efforts to restore my physical body. Three months after beginning to desist, I came back to the Catholic church after a friend told me about Reintegrative Therapy™ for those seeking to diminish same-sex attractions. I discovered there is no "born this way" and that the church was not hateful and bigoted as I'd been led to believe. My mental state today is vastly different from my former life. I no longer suffer from debilitating depression, thanks to my awakening to a new life in Christ. In hindsight, I wish there had been more mainstream dissenting information freely available, especially within Christian churches, the medical community, and the political arena. It is my hope to one day see a paradigm shift wherein medical science embraces the growing evidence that refutes the dangerous procedures and drugs endorsed by WPATH and wherein the so-called "transgender medical" industry openly refutes procedures and drugs to identify as the opposite sex, calling them ineffective or harmful, as evidence supports.

LIVING AS A TRANS WOMAN

JEREMY TODAY

ERIN EVERITT

ADVOCATES PROTECTING CHILDREN
advocatesprotectingchildren.org

"

No one, not even my mother, knew that my longing to be a boy, a budding transgender identity, was based upon my desire to keep my body from being sexually violated.

ERIN EVERITT

Between kindergarten and first grade, my brother and I were abducted by two men and taken to a public restroom. I was brutally sexually assaulted, but my brother was not. Filled with shame, I never told anyone what happened. In my child's mind, I thought being a boy would prevent me from ever being assaulted again by men. So, to protect myself, I dressed in my brother's clothes and did my best to act like boys. I got in trouble for being too aggressive, both verbally and physically, and I even practiced peeing standing up. I thought if I could master this skill, I could "pass" as a boy. Eventually, I cultivated same-sex relationships while pretending to be a boy.

In my child's mind, I thought being a boy would prevent me from ever being assaulted again by men.

In the first grade, my teacher asked the school psychologist to evaluate me; she could tell something was terribly wrong. The psychologist then told my mother that I wanted to be a boy. To alleviate my hatred for my female body, she made some simple recommendations for my mother and my teachers, including reinforcing positive ideas of being a woman, exposing me to strong, talented women, putting me in activities with other girls, like Brownies or Bluebirds, and discouraging me from wearing my brother's hand-me-downs. No one, not even my mother, knew that my longing to be a boy, a budding transgender identity, was based upon my desire to keep my body from being sexually violated, and it took years of therapy before I even understood the connection.

Though therapy helped me understand the root cause of my childhood gender confusion, it did not address the brokenness and pain that resulted from my early childhood trauma. As a result, I engaged in same-sex relationships as a teenager. Later, I realized that my same-sex attraction was the result of my fear of men and my desire to feel safe. Again, therapy helped me address my fear, but it did not address the core problem: the trauma of childhood sexual assault. As a result, I was drawn to pornography, where I made and posted more than 400 videos on Pornhub as a solo performer. Men would give me encouragement, thanking me for acting out their sexual fantasies and telling me how

ERIN LIVING AS A BOY

ERIN TODAY

wonderful I was. I even had a therapist encouraging me to develop this new "career." He likened me to being a social worker for men who had never been sexually fulfilled.

During this season, I was invited to speak at an Eagle Forum conference about my childhood gender dysphoria. A proud leftist atheist, I disagreed with almost everything they espoused, yet they welcomed me anyway. While there, I felt God's love reflected by those in attendance. *If they knew I was making a living making porn,* I thought, *they would ask me to leave in disgust.* But when I confessed to a number of people, rather than reject me, they responded with God's love. After my presentation, during the Q&A session, a woman from Alabama came to the mic and said, "I don't have a question, but wanted to tell you that even though you don't believe in God, He believes in you." God's love began to soften my heart, and shortly after I returned home, I surrendered my life to Jesus and asked Him to be my Lord and Savior. Filled with peace for the first time in my life, I realized that all my brokenness, from my childhood gender conflict to my same-sex relationships to porn, was because I was trying to fix something deep within myself that only Jesus could heal. I am so thankful that my school psychologist put me on a healing path. I am grateful to other therapists who helped me understand that my perceived "transgender" identity was a result of the sexual assault, not because I was born in the wrong body. But mostly, I'm thankful for Jesus. When I accepted Him as my Savior, I realized that

"

Today I know who I am: God's adopted and much-loved daughter.

I had been searching all my life for an identity—first as a girl identifying as a boy, then as a lesbian, then as a porn star. God delivered me from these destructive and false identities and miraculously healed me from the brokenness I'd lived with most of my life. Today, I know who I am: God's adopted and much-loved daughter, and I pray that those who have internal conflict over their sex or sexual feelings will find healing and identity in Him.

EDMUND SMITH

EDMUND LIVING/DRESSING AS A GIRL UNTIL AGE 7

EDMUND TODAY

"

Twenty-nine years later, there has been no turning back! Today, I continue in full-time ministry along with my wife, and we travel all over Malaysia.

EDMUND SMITH

Born into an unhappy religious family in Malaysia, I grew up feeling that I was a girl trapped in a boy's body. In fact, from the time I was four years old, I remember experiencing confusion about my sex. Until I was about seven, I lived and dressed as a girl, but because attending school as a girl was not an option in my country, I was compelled to dress more androgynously from ages seven to 21. I had rejected myself because my father seemed clearly disappointed that I was born a boy (his fourth son), not his long-awaited daughter. It was no secret that my father preferred girls to boys, and when my sister Helga (Dad's precious jewel) was born, he showered her (and even my female cousins) with the affection that I craved.

Because I didn't know the difference between love and sex, I started having sex with men at the young age of 13.

Growing up, I was thrilled whenever any boys gave me the slightest attention—especially when they wanted to have any kind of relationship with me, and I believed this fueled my same-sex attraction. Because I didn't know the difference between love and sex, I started having sex with men at the young age of 13. That's also the time at which I began to explore the idea of undergoing surgical interventions to look like a woman. After reading that anyone over 21 is eligible in Thailand, I began to dream, plan, and save money for surgery.

Even though I was struggling with my identity, I still somehow knew that my calling in this life was to help society's marginalized. It made sense; I myself was a marginalized individual living in a mainstream world. At 13, I volunteered as a community worker with the Catholic nuns running adult literacy projects for the illiterate adults in the immigrant settlement in my hometown in Malaysia. Then, in 1988, when I was about 18 years old, The Salvation Army employed me as a community worker, working closely with people who were mentally challenged. Years later, that placement hugely impacted my life, as it was the place where I was first guided into a relationship with the Lord Jesus Christ.

Around the time that I began working at The Salvation Army, I also fell in love for the very first time. He was a handsome bisexual man who actually guided me out of my "trans woman" identity. He showed me, slowly but surely, that

> “
>
> I had rejected myself because my father seemed clearly disappointed that I was born a boy (his fourth son), not his long-awaited daughter.

I did not need to be a woman for him to love me. By the time I was 21 years old, I had moved from identifying as a “trans woman” to a homosexual man, during which time I ended up living a stereotypically wild, gay lifestyle. After breaking up with him, I experienced uncountable one-night stands (with all kinds of men, young and old) and two other long-term relationships. I also performed sex for money, was raped, and participated in orgies, all in my desperate pursuit of Mister Right. Because I experienced such pain and uncertainty, I eventually walked away from gay culture in 1994, weary from living a meaningless life. I was 24 years old.

At the end of 1994, as I turned away from gay identity, God used two special women to help bring healing into my painful past: Jenny, a Salvation Army worker, who eventually became a pastor, and Amanda (who is now my wife), who is also a pastor today serving alongside me in ministry. God used Amanda and Jenny powerfully to hold my hand, love me, and pray with me. The transition from being gay to no longer identifying as gay was truly tough, and I couldn’t have done it without them. As my life took a turn, however, I became extremely excited about discovering Jesus, serving Him, living my life for Him, and making the world around me a better place in which to live. Twenty-nine years later, there has been no turning back! Today, I continue in full-time ministry along with my wife, and we travel all over Malaysia—and even to other countries—teaching and ministering in churches about spirituality and sexual redemption. We are the proud parents of two wonderful children, Angelica and Ethan. Becoming a parent was once only a dream for me, but today this beautiful dream is a reality thanks to the Almighty God!

EDMUND PRESENTING ANDROGYNOUSLY

EDMUND AND HIS WIFE

BILLY BURLEIGH

BILLY TODAY

BILLY LIVING AS BILLIE

FREEDOM IN CHRIST MINISTRIES INTERNATIONAL
freedominchrist.org

"

No matter how many surgeries I had, every time I looked in the mirror, I saw a man staring back at me.

BILLY BURLEIGH

I had many difficulties as a child. In addition to being unusually skinny, I had a speech impediment and learning difficulties. In fact, I didn't learn how to read until about the fifth grade. I was very uncoordinated and lacked athletic skills, which caused me to be teased by classmates and friends. When I was in the first grade, I remember having the recurring thought that God had made a mistake. I would pray before going to bed, "God, please make me a girl before I wake up." To make matters worse, when I was in the sixth grade, I was sexually molested. Scared and ashamed, I hated my private parts and wished they were gone!

I continued to struggle secretly, feeling like I was actually a girl throughout childhood. An expert at stuffing my emotions, I managed to avoid dealing with my confusion until I fell in love with a young lady in college. Overwhelmed by feelings of love, I knew I had to deal with these confusing feelings of dysphoria. My sister helped me find a sexuality therapist, and I also started using the university's resources to research "transgenderism." Though I desired to be a "normal man," the messages I received were overwhelming: The only way to overcome my dysphoria was to change my body to conform to my inner identity. Still hopeful that I could live as a man, I married my college sweetheart and continued to seek therapy. But after five or six years of agony—and a failed marriage—I told my therapist that I wanted to identify as a woman. Struggling with depression, I was willing to try anything, and she affirmed my decision.

As a child I thought that, by "being a girl," my psychological needs would be fulfilled. But that was wrong.

I changed my name from Billy to Billie and began taking a testosterone blocker and estrogen. Three years later, I had my first surgery—a penile inversion, an Adam's apple shave, and a brow shave. Afterwards, the doctor and nurses had difficulty stopping the bleeding from my new "vagina." They packed my artificial vagina with gauze and put a sandbag on my lower abdomen in an effort to stop the bleeding. But it would not stop, and they had to administer a blood transfusion and plasma. Over time, I jumped through all the hoops and did everything I was supposed to do to try to change my sex. I had cosmetic surgeries to look more like a woman, but no matter how many surgeries I had, every time I looked in the mirror, I saw a man staring back at me.

Ironically, I had married a second time prior to these surgeries. Though my wife and I both identified as heterosexual, we presented as a lesbian couple after my surgery. We loved each other deeply, but our marriage couldn't withstand the stress, and she eventually divorced me seven years later. I realized I had more problems than ever before. Changing my body had not resolved my internal conflict and had not made me happy. Instead, I was left with countless scars, two broken marriages, and drained financial resources. Depression began to set back in, and once again, I was searching for answers. So, I moved back to Baton Rouge, Louisiana, to gain the support of my family. Desperate for change, I also cried out to God. The day I made the decision to surrender my life and my problems to Jesus, I actually heard him say, "Now, I have some clay to work with."

Slowly but surely, as I began to seek the things of God, circumstances in my life began to change radically. I returned to church and began spending time in Bible study and prayer. The more I learned about spiritual warfare and biblical identity, the clearer my mind became. It was as if someone had turned on a light bulb. As I read the books *Reclaiming Surrendered Ground: Protecting Your Family from Spiritual Attacks* by Jim Logan and *Victory Over the Darkness* and *The Bondage Breaker* by Neil T. Anderson, I had epiphany after epiphany. Within a year, at age 38, I began making choices to go back to identifying as a man. The entire process took about two or three years, and during that time, I changed all my documents and returned to my original identity as Billy.

> “
>
> I had a number of childhood issues that the mental health professionals failed to uncover and adequately address.

YOUNG BILLY

I am now 55 years old. My thoughts are clear, and I am free of the mental turmoil I had as a kid and growing up. I am happily married to a woman. I have two beautiful stepdaughters and best of all, I have peace of mind. With the benefit of age and experience, I now realize the procedures I underwent as a young man failed me in several areas. First, none of my mental health counselors ever told me that all people have a continuing need for acceptance, significance, and security. As a child, I thought that, by "being a girl," my psychological needs would be fulfilled. But that was wrong. Second, the mental health professionals simply assumed that the only way I could be mentally healthy was to convince myself that I should have been, and therefore was, a woman. But that was also wrong. The many surgical procedures and drugs they encouraged left me worse off than when I began.

BILLY LIVING AS BILLIE

Third, I had a number of childhood issues that the mental health professionals failed to uncover and adequately address. Had those issues (a speech impediment, a learning disability, and childhood sexual abuse) been dealt with properly, I may have never gone down the expensive and painful road on which I traveled.

I have great compassion for children and teenagers who feel this same inner incongruence. They look to their parents and healthcare professionals for guidance. Even as an adult, I relied on the mental health counseling I received while deciding whether to change my presentation from male to female. But in my experience, the mental health profession is so quick to promote identifying as the opposite sex that surgical procedures and drugs are promoted as the only real solution for those struggling. My mental health professionals led me to make a horrible mistake. This experience has led me to question whether most mental health professionals have adequate training to make the right recommendations for still-developing children and teenagers.

TODAY

LINDA SEILER

RESTORY MINISTRIES
restoryministries.org

LINDA SEILER NOW

"

I eventually broke off that relationship, realizing my fantasy of being a man who slept with women would never fill the deep void in my soul.

LINDA SEILER

From my earliest memory, I wanted to be a boy instead of a girl. Somehow, I just knew that if I had male genitalia, my life would be complete. As a child, I prayed repeatedly for God to make me into a boy and became obsessed with my pursuit. However, I never told my family. Though I was a tomboy growing up, no one ever knew the depth of my struggles. It was my little secret that I kept for decades. Around fourth grade, I heard about "gender transition" surgeries and vowed I would have the operation as soon as I was old enough and had the money. About the same time, some playmates introduced me to pornography, which developed into sexual addictions that would span the next 20+ years. Unbeknownst to my parents, I would spend hours alone in my room feeding my sexual fantasies, always visualizing myself as the male counterpart rather than the female.

In junior high, when all the other girls were interested in makeup and boys, I found myself attracted to women—especially older teachers who were strong yet nurturing. I desperately wanted to be held and comforted by a woman, which then progressed into sexual fantasies. Around seventh grade, I started to consider the logistical difficulties of having surgery to look like a man. Where would I get the money? How would I tell my family? You can't just be Linda one day and David the next. I considered running away as soon as I reached adulthood to have the surgery without ever telling my family, but I loved my family, and I didn't want to live without them. At that point, I made a conscious decision to try to conform to society's expectation of me to look more like a girl to fit in. But inside, I still longed deeply to be a man.

When I wore dresses on special occasions... I always felt like I was dressing in drag.

I committed my life to Jesus during my junior year in high school, but within days, I began doubting my salvation experience because my struggles didn't go away like I thought they would. Yet, I knew Jesus had done something in my heart, and I wanted to follow Him. I got involved with my church youth group and, for the first time in my life, felt like I had friends who loved me. But the more I tried to conform to being a girl, the more I wanted to be a boy. When I wore dresses on special occasions, for instance, I always felt like I was dressing in drag.

During college, I continued living a double life, participating in campus ministries but still silently struggling with confusion about my sex and with homosexuality. Then, when I was a senior, I confessed to my campus pastor the secret I had kept for 21 years. Before talking to him, I seriously

LINDA EXPERIENCING GENDER DYSPHORIA

LINDA NOW

considered suicide as a way out, but I knew that would devastate my family, and I couldn't do that to them. I expected my pastor to react with shock, horror, or condemnation. Instead, he responded to me in love, assuring me he was committed to finding me the help I needed. For the first time, I discovered that being completely transparent with another person was very healing. That day in 1994 was the first step in what would be my 11-year journey to freedom.

The next decade was full of ups and downs as I sought healing by reading books, listening to teachings, and meeting with multiple counselors—even those from ex-gay ministries. It was a slow process, as there were not many resources at that time to help women struggling with issues like mine. However, because I thirsted so deeply for nurture, I seemed to get worse before I got better. I ended up in a sexual relationship with another woman from my church. Realizing my fantasy of being a man who slept with women would never fill the deep void in my soul, I eventually ended our relationship.

It was as if I could literally feel His hands holding my heart.

As I continued to pursue healing, the Lord put a spiritual mentor in my life who was only a few years older than me but spiritually much more mature. I was deeply attracted to her, yet my struggles didn't faze her, and she began to invest in me relationally in a wholesome way. I found myself wanting to be just like her (much like a daughter might want to emulate her mother). She helped me buy more feminine clothes and gave me advice concerning makeup and mannerisms. Yet, though my outward appearance began to change, inwardly I still believed the lie that it was better to be a man.

Then, in the fall of 2005, the Lord led me to meet with an inner healing prayer counselor. Over the course of a week, we spent hours praying through a lifetime of deep emotional wounds that were at the root of my issues. I forgave those who hurt me, let go of bitterness, renounced inner vows, and repented for my wrong responses toward those who had wounded me. I embraced the cross, and we closed every spiritual door I had opened to give the enemy grounds to influence my life. I wept as the Lord spoke graciously to me; it was as if I could literally feel His hands holding my heart. After that powerful encounter with God, I had a newfound contentment in being a woman and was miraculously set free from my sexual addictions. As I continued to walk out my healing, I eventually started experiencing genuine attraction toward men. It was as if I was going through delayed puberty in my mid-30s, which was both awkward and thrilling. God had transformed me from the inside out and accomplished the impossible. I still feel like I'm living a dream.

I'm grateful for all the pastors, counselors, faithful friends, and especially my supportive parents who walked with me during the healing process. The 11-year journey toward transformation was totally worth it. The length of the journey itself has given me empathy for those who are currently struggling to break free from similar issues and sometimes feel hopeless. Healing from sexual brokenness is rarely instantaneous—it's often more like peeling back layers of an onion one at a time—but if we hold fast to the truth of God's Word and determine never to give up, we will experience transformation to the point that the sin that once characterized our lives ceases to dominate us. God promised: "Such were some of you" (1 Corinthians 6:11).

"

I started seeing a Christian counselor, attended conferences and found some books. These were all very instrumental in bringing about change and healing in my life.

JEFF JOHNSTON

At five years old, I engaged in sexual play and was introduced to sexual things by other young boys in my neighborhood. That caused me to pull back from connecting with other boys, because I didn't want that to happen again. So, I tended to connect more with girls. In junior high, I discovered pornography and got hooked on it. I felt shame and guilt, afraid that someone would find out what I was doing. I became even more disturbed when my fascination with pornography began to shift from women to men. But I worked to maintain an outer image of being fine for years, even as the sexual addiction and homosexual attraction increased.

Then in my early 20s I went to Australia as a missionary for several years. When I came back, I was working with a high school group and was reaching the end of my rope. The contrast between struggling intensely with my sexuality and being involved in the church was extremely difficult.

But during that time, I went to a conference called "Hope and Healing for the Homosexual." It was the first time I had heard anyone talk about potential reasons behind same-sex attraction or that it was possible to leave homosexuality.

That conference was a turning point for me; within a week, I started going to a support group for people who also wanted to leave homosexuality. I had kept this part of my life hidden for years, but slowly I began talking to friends and family about my struggle. Where I feared rejection, I usually found compassion and concern. I also started seeing a Christian counselor, attended conferences about healing sexuality and found some books on the issue. These were all very instrumental in bringing about change and healing in my life.

Although I started out strong in my journey out of homosexuality, I went through a period of time when I really questioned my faith and my identity as a Christian. I started going to clubs and having sex with men I had just met. There was a lot of talk about HIV/AIDS during that time, and I knew my choices were very unsafe.

Finally, I made a return to my faith and to the Church. Instead of pursuing a role in leadership, I just focused on pursuing healthy, non-sexual relationships with men. I had a mentor, and I got involved in weekly accountability relationship groups. I had guy friends who loved and accepted me where I was, but who would also call me out when I did things that weren't good for me. And I realized that my struggle wasn't that different from some of their struggles. Those relationships were incredibly healing and transformative for me.

A few years later, I began leading a group at my church, and a young lady came, who I thought was cute. Judy and I ended up dating and then getting married. We are still married and have a healthy relationship and have three sons together. Our oldest is 27, and we have twins who are 24.

JEFF JOHNSTON

FOCUS ON THE FAMILY'S
Daily Citizen
dailycitizen.focusonthefamily.com

KIM ZEMBER

OVERCOME / *overcomemin.com*

“

In contrast to what most people would think, I actually found great freedom [to stop acting on my same-sex desires].

KIM ZEMBER

I started having homosexual desires in high school and began acting on them when I was 17. For many years, I hid them from my family and friends because I felt so much shame and guilt about them, which came from a deep feeling I had personally that I wasn't meant to live a lesbian lifestyle. I was living a double life, and it tormented me.

I lived that way for years, dating girl after girl and hiding it from everyone I cared about. I ended up marrying a man whom I respected, but was not in love with. Then I cheated on him with a woman. After that happened, I was basically forced to come out with the life I was choosing to live. The people close to me accepted me and were supportive although I felt in my heart that they believed, as I did deep down, that my lifestyle wasn't good for me. Going from relationship to relationship, I was never at peace in my heart, and I finally hit rock bottom when one of my girlfriends cheated on me.

For the first time, my life felt full.

At that point, I realized that I was in a vicious cycle of relationships that weren't fulfilling for me. Even though everyone around me supported my lifestyle and told me it was OK, I felt deeply convinced that I needed to make big changes if I wanted different results in my life.

I became so desperate that I finally decided to surrender everything about the way I had been living and ask for God's help. From that moment on, the heaviness I had been living in for many years was lifted. I began reading different books about sexuality and what the Bible says about it. I also attended seminars and met with a priest who helped me process sexuality through a faith-based perspective. I also committed not to date at all for a time. These things brought peace to my heart that I had been searching for, and for the first time, my life felt full, like I was living out my true identity.

It was not easy to stop acting on my same-sex desires, but I had the support I needed to choose not to. In contrast to what most people would think, I actually found great freedom in putting up those boundaries for myself. I am also now free from the anxiety, depression, and duplicity that were continually present in my past lifestyle. I now walk in an authenticity that I didn't know was possible.

Kim's heart also overflows with joy and love for children in Ethiopia. Visit her ministry at **www.unforgottenfaces.org.**

"

After deciding I wanted to come out of the lesbian lifestyle, I met Garry, who is now my husband. We have been married 16 years, and we have two children.

MELISSA INGRAHAM

WIFE TO GARRY / PAGE 112

From the outside, my life looked pretty perfect. I was attending a private university and was in a long-term relationship with a guy. But inside, I was growing more and more depressed, with a huge sense of emptiness. I felt confused and unsatisfied, so I began to question my sexuality.

My senior year of college I began a lesbian relationship with a woman. At first I thought, *This is what I've been looking for my whole life,* but then I experienced a lot of internal conflict between feeling like it was right and a nagging sense that it was wrong. I felt a lot of shame, and I had no peace. Our relationship was very intense, but short-lived. She ended things quickly, and I was devastated.

My life today is 100 times better than it was then.

At that point it felt like all my relationships had come crashing down on me, and I reached my lowest point. I felt like I was dying inside. So, I began to ask God for help and to look for help externally, as well.

I was nervous to tell my mom and twin sister that I thought I was gay because they were Christians and I thought they would respond harshly. Instead, they both responded by saying, "We don't think this is God's best for you, but we love you, anyway." My sister invited me to a Christian conference, and I went with her. While I was there, I came to believe that just because I felt something, that didn't make it right.

I began to read books and web pages about healthy sexuality, which were very helpful in providing me with a private way to get information that I needed since I still felt a lot of shame in the beginning. I then joined a local ministry that was helping people deal with unwanted sexual attractions. That ministry provided support for me in my process by helping me deal with brokenness in my family and helping me to extend forgiveness. A part of that ministry was joining a paid support group, where I learned how to build healthy relationships. I also sought counseling, and attended conferences. Each of those things was instrumental in my healing process.

My life today is 100 times better than it was then. About five years after deciding I wanted to come out of a lesbian lifestyle, I met Garry, who is now my husband. We have been married 17 years, and we have two children. My husband and I have a great sex life, and my level of same-sex attraction is extremely small compared to what it was.

MELISSA INGRAHAM

LOVE AND TRUTH NETWORK / *loveandtruthnetwork.com*

GARRY INGRAHAM

LOVE AND TRUTH NETWORK
loveandtruthnetwork.com

"

I was able to find solid, legitimate support that helped me determine my sexuality in a way that lined up with my faith and desires.

GARRY INGRAHAM

HUSBAND TO MELISSA / PAGE 111

My life as a gay man was pretty chaotic. There were certainly some high points when I was living in sexuality and bartending at a gay bar, but for the most part, the lows were extremely low, and there were many of them. The more I continued to live in homosexuality and identify as a gay man, the more unstable my life became.

I was using a lot of alcohol, sex and other types of distractions in order to just cope with life. I would say that my life was going out of control. I experienced a lot of depression and anxiety. I didn't really want to commit suicide. Somehow, I wished I could simply not exist.

Eventually, I got to a point where the euphoria of coming out, leaving Bible college, finding my first gay bar, and feeling like I had finally found my people started to lift. It was almost two years in, and I was starting to feel hollow. My desire had always been to find Mr. Right and settle down. When that didn't happen, and I was with countless numbers of guys, it was anything but what I had signed up for. I realized there was no hope or joy. There was nothing in it for me.

I grew up going to church, but I had experienced some negative aspects. Even as an adult, I have at times. But I started to have a desire to rediscover God in a way that was very different from what I used to know. The desire didn't have anything to do with wanting to change my sexuality. (At that point, it felt immutable.) All I knew was I needed to turn the reins over to somebody else.

I wouldn't trade my worst day today for my best day then.

The journey was painful, but good. I started to go to different conferences annually. Those were transformational. I learned from people who were dealing with some of the same issues, and it gave me insight into how some of them had developed in my own life. I wasn't told exactly how it happened, but it helped me put the dots together and realize, *Oh, this makes a lot of sense.*

Books and recordings were also pivotal for me. They really gave me hope for what I was beginning to pursue and were a big part of what brought the change. Counseling also played a crucial part. I was on a pretty desperate journey, but I was able to find solid, legitimate support that helped me determine my sexuality in a way that lined up with my faith and desires.

I've been happily married 17 years now to my wife, Melissa. Today I sometimes say, "I wouldn't trade my worst day today for my best day then." It's true. There's so much stability, love, and growth in my life now, and there has been for a long time. I'm so thankful.

"

Today I live knowing that what once brought me the most shame is completely taken away by a God who didn't avoid my pain or questions.

GABRIEL PAGAN

I used to be very depressed and constantly paranoid of what people thought about me. I explored sexuality in high school after being exposed to sexual activity and pornography as a kid. Acting out through masturbation and webcams became an obsessive habit to which I lost all control. It got to the point that I was acting out in public what I was seeing on screens.

I was depressed, but now I'm full of joy.

This brought me to my lowest point. I wanted to kill myself. I was unaware that people were praying for me. Because they were praying, I felt motivated to change my life. Someone reached out to me on social media and shared Jesus with me. I accepted Jesus Christ in my driveway and the Holy Spirit fell on me like fire, which brought me through a series of encounters. I went through a prayer ministry and saw Jesus holding me the first time I was touched inappropriately, and I told the Lord that I would never sleep with another man if I had His presence like that forever.

Twelve years later and I'm free from being bound to same-sex attractions. I'm happy and living a wild life of adventure following Jesus Christ. Today, I live knowing that what once brought me the most shame is completely taken away by a God who didn't avoid my pain or questions. I serve as a pastor at my local church and lead people through inner healing prayer sessions. My greatest joy is seeing Jesus crush unbelief by stepping into people's pain and watching them encounter the God who kept me from ending my own life. I was addicted, but now I'm free. I was depressed, but now I'm full of joy. I was full of hate, but now I'm moved by love. I've been married to my beautiful wife since 2019, and we have three wonderful little boys together. I love my new life.

GABRIEL PAGAN

THE RAINBOW JOURNEY
https://linktr.ee/rainbowprophet

“

At the core of all of this has been a belief that God’s power is real and active today.

RODGER GASKIN

I was born “that way,” or at least that is the way it felt. For most of my life I was only sexually attracted to men. While I longed for both emotional and sexual intimacy with a man, I also felt as though I didn’t belong with other men and that I was a foreigner. At the same time, most of my life I have been surrounded by men who valued and pursued non-sexual relationships with me. They didn’t see me as an outsider or as less-than. Many of them knew I struggled with homosexuality, but this didn’t deter them from caring for me. Yet I couldn’t connect with them. I was deeply uncomfortable with them while longing to be with them.

In my 20s, I started to explore ways to better integrate my faith and sexuality. I began reading books on the topic, and I attended a conference for people with unwanted sexual attractions.

I saw a therapist and worked on many issues, including childhood trauma and depression. And I spent time, often at these conferences or other gatherings, with men and women who had experienced significant change in their sexual orientation.

These resources gave me a vision and hope that real change was possible and that it wasn’t a fraudulent claim. At the core of all of this has been a belief that God’s power is real and active today. With this, I have a personal commitment to the belief that sexual relationships are intended to be expressed between a man and a woman only.

At this point in my life, I have experienced magnificent change in the quality of my life. The greatest change has been in how I relate to other men. While I previously felt like an outsider and like I didn’t belong, I am now very comfortable in my relationships with other men.

I am confident and secure in who I am.

Amazingly, I also find myself sexually attracted to women; what an oddly wonderful experience. With this, there has been a change in my sexual attraction towards men. The more comfortable and closer I have come relationally with other men, the less sexual attraction I have for men.

As I have addressed areas of confusion, trauma, and fear, the power of homosexual desire has lessened. My attention has gone from dealing with the attraction itself to dealing with the root issues behind it. The overall quality of my life has improved, and I am confident and secure in who I am as a human who is fully male. I continue to grow as a man and as a follower of Jesus.

RODGER GASKIN

DEREK PAUL

IDENTIFY MINISTRIES
identifyministries.org

“

I am sexually attracted to my wife and more content in my marriage than I could have ever dreamed.

DEREK PAUL

I experienced same-sex attraction for most of my life. I was born into a pastor's family and had a traditional upbringing that I cherished. However, because of some early ongoing harassment from male peers and a gymnastics coach, some intrusive medical exams, and less than optimal family dynamics, I began to experience gender confusion and same-sex attraction as a small child. In high school, I became very involved in the worlds of theater and competitive cheerleading. These atmospheres and peer groups were enjoyable, but they exposed me to lifestyles that led me to question my identity and purpose.

I have peace and no longer feel conflicted.

By college, the constant inner turmoil of same-sex attraction and my conservative Christian worldview came to a crossroad, and I decided to plan my exit strategy and enter the gay lifestyle. Simultaneously, I met a Christian woman whose life had been changed through Jesus to a level I hadn't yet seen. She was the first Christian to suggest I could seek recovery because of her own experience with God's power and love.

Later I found support and discipleship in an accountability partner and a local support group. Because of the changes in my relationship with God and my supportive Christian community, I felt secure enough to challenge perspectives and worldviews that had gone unquestioned in my heart.

Today, the Christian woman who was my friend has since become my wife. We have been married for 18 years and have 3 children. I am sexually attracted to her and more content in my marriage than I could have ever dreamed. I am no longer bound to sexualize men; I have peace and no longer feel conflicted. My relationships with family and friends are full and enjoyable, and I have gained a lifestyle that surpassed all my expectations.

"

I now have a reconciled relationship with my family and the privilege of helping others know that change is possible.

LUIS RUIZ

I always knew I wanted to marry a woman and have a family of my own. So when I realized in my childhood that I was attracted to the same sex, I felt my dream might not be possible. I fell prey to the world's narrative that "you are born gay," which left me feeling confused and hopeless. Too fearful to share my same-sex feelings with my parents and my church, I felt disconnected from God and my family because of the tension between my desires and my beliefs.

I chose to leave the gay lifestyle to pursue my true identity.

While I served in the US Army, I secretly explored gay clubs where I medicated my pain with partying, drugs and sex with other men. I wanted to drown out the pain of not feeling attracted to women. Throughout those years, I continually felt there had to be more to life than what I was living. When I got out of the Army, I was depressed and alone.

On June 12, 2016, I was celebrating my birthday at Pulse Nightclub in Orlando when a shooter entered the building and opened fire. After losing many of my friends and being taken to the hospital for wounds sustained during the shooting, I came to learn I was HIV positive. At that moment I dropped to my knees and wept. I wanted to live a healthier life, one that was not centered around sex and damaging behavior.

I started going to a church where I received pastoral care and began connecting with a supportive faith community. I began to fall in love with the faith of my childhood. These resources allowed me to build healthy relationships and pursue a relationship with God. I chose to leave the gay lifestyle to pursue my true identity in Jesus. I now live a life free of depression, anxiety and fear, having a reconciled relationship with my family and the privilege of helping others know that change is possible.

LUIS RUIZ

Orlando Pulse Nightclub Shooting Survivor

FEARLESS IDENTITY
fearlessidentity.co

"

I became so miserable that I started looking for other ways to fill the void in my soul, including drugs and bulimia.

JANET BOYNES

The trauma and pain from my childhood, which was filled with physical and sexual abuse, led me into a series of broken lesbian relationships. Before I entered into a lesbian lifestyle, I had been a Christian and was engaged to be married. My fiancé was gone a lot, and I hated being alone, so I spent a lot of time with a woman from work. This interaction opened the door to my first sexual encounter with a woman, leading me away from God and my fiancé and into a life of lesbianism.

I had finally found what I was looking for.

Each time I tried to return to God, I felt pulled to hold onto that lifestyle. I even toyed with the idea of getting a sex change to make the relationships more "normal" but couldn't bring myself to go through with it. I became so miserable that I started looking for other ways to fill the void in my soul, including drugs and eventually bulimia.

One October morning in a grocery store I encountered a woman who invited me to her church. I knew right then and there that our meeting was not a coincidence and that this was a new beginning for me. Through this encounter in 1998, God intervened in my life and called me out of the lesbian lifestyle. With the help of people at Maple Grove Assemblies of God in Minnesota, I never looked back. I had finally found what I was looking for. After living a lesbian lifestyle for 14 years, I found freedom through Jesus Christ.

In 2006, Janet Boynes Ministries was incorporated, with the mission of reaching those who are trapped in the struggle that I once found myself in, and on April 20, 2018, I was ordained as a pastor by the General Council of the Assemblies of God.

BEFORE

JANET BOYNES

JANET BOYNES
janetboynesministries.com

TODAY

DAVID RASMUSSEN

"

I joined a group of married men who also struggled with homosexuality, and we all encouraged each other and shared our stories.

DAVID RASMUSSEN

Diane and I went to high school together and planned on getting married. I didn't have same-sex attractions until college, but at college, I discovered pornography and homosexuality. I was acting out, going to parks, bookstores, restrooms, and bathhouses. I didn't know anything about homosexuality. It wasn't talked about, and it was a shameful thing. So I hid it. Diane suspected, and before we got married, I had to tell her I had an STD that I had gotten from a man. Miraculously, she still agreed to marry me. We cried and hugged, and the wedding went on. We both went into marriage thinking it would be a cure.

We learned quickly that marriage was not a cure. We were able to be intimate, but I started living a double life and continued acting out. I put on a facade that everything was fine, but inside I was a mess. I experienced a lot of guilt and shame, but I didn't know I was a sex addict. I felt that what I was doing was wrong, but I didn't know what to do about it. Eventually, I was committing adultery, which made things even worse.

I didn't have same-sex attractions until college.

At one of my lowest points, I was at a bathhouse, and an unattractive older man approached me. He asked me to have sex, offering to pay me $20. I refused, and he asked me to hug him for $20. I gave him a hug and told him to keep his money. When I got home, I looked in the mirror, and I saw that old man. And I saw my future life: no wife, no children, all alone, having to pay for touch. I started to cry and got on my knees, desperate to change. Finally, I became desperate enough that I pursued change, and I started a relationship with God.

I started building healthy relationships with men for the first time in my life, and I learned a lot about being a man, husband, and father through them. I also shared about my struggle publicly at church, and everyone stood and applauded my courage. I also found out about a program that helps people with unwanted same-sex attractions, and they gave me books on the topic. Most importantly, I joined a group of married men who also struggled with homosexuality, and we all encouraged each other and shared our stories.

It is so nice not to be living the double life I did in my youth. I am authentic and let people see who I really am. I don't have to carry the secrets and burdens anymore.

Diane, my wife and best friend, passed away June 17th, 2023. I would not be where I am today without her encouragement and willingness to walk alongside me during the change journey I was on. Despite my mistakes and my struggle, Diane chose to stay with me through it all. She chose to forgive me. We went on the journey of healing together.

“

The gay identity I once explored had only limited my ability to fully express myself.

CALEB BOGGAN

I've spent my whole life knowing that I was different and that I would never fit in. It wasn't until third grade, when a classmate called me "gay," that I began to question whether or not something was wrong with me. This "gay" label started a pattern in my life of questioning, believing I was broken, and constantly feeling on the outside of masculinity. With a flare for the dramatic and a love of all things Disney, Broadway, and glitter, I felt there was no place for my version of masculinity and even began to question whether I should have been a woman. I stuffed away my emotions and ignored my heart.

Eventually, though, I felt like I had no choice but to accept this identity that others had placed on me and began to own a gay identity. So, I turned my back on my convictions and began to explore whether this gay identity fit me. After a long time of venturing down this road, I never found the fulfillment I was looking for in men. I realized how miserable I'd become and how much of myself I'd lost.

I decided that something had to change and began the journey of rediscovering who I was. I discovered that I didn't have to be gay to be fully me—glitter and all. I eventually found a Christian community where I could be authentic and be open about my struggle so that I could discover for myself the truth about who I was, who God was, and how I wanted to live.

Through open and honest conversations with a few trusted people, I experienced acceptance in my expression of masculinity. If that had not been available to me, I would have been completely alone in the journey. I also realized that God was so much better and kinder than I'd ever known.

Now I feel comfortable in who I am as a man.

Today, I'm more freely myself than I ever imagined possible! Being me, fully male and fully alive, is how I find joy and happiness. The gay identity I once explored had only limited my ability to fully express myself. Now I feel comfortable in who I am as a man. I have been on a beautiful journey to rediscover the unique aspects of my identity and personality that are part of my expression of masculinity. I can be creative, love Broadway, and have emotions, and none of this makes me any less of a man. I don't struggle with same-sex attraction the way I used to. I experience attraction to women and enjoy deep, rewarding friendship with men. I have so much hope and vision for my life and, specifically, for marrying a woman and starting a family of my own one day. I'm the happiest I've ever been and living life more fulfilled than I ever dreamed was possible.

CALEB BOGGAN

CHANGED MOVEMENT
changedmovement.com

JENNIFER THORNE

JENS CHAT ON THAT / *jenschatonthat.blogspot.com*

"

I pursued growth in my Christian faith, and it began to change me and the way I viewed life.

JENNIFER THORNE

I didn't know how to relate to other women, and I didn't know how to relate to men, either. Growing up I'd had no close friends who were girls. I was a tomboy and played with the boys. So, it felt as though I had gone from having no relational connections with women whatsoever to having sexual relationships with them. I felt that men were unsafe, and I couldn't connect with them emotionally.

I started living a lesbian lifestyle when I was a teenager, and I was sexually promiscuous. When I was 24, I became close friends with a woman who was unwilling to get sexually involved with me because I did not share her Christian faith. I was miserable and in an emotional downward spiral. Thankfully, some family members offered me some much-needed unconditional love and were there for me to help answer my questions.

My cousin gave me a book asserting the reality of God, and it spoke deeply to me personally. I prayed to become a Christian, but secretly my motivation was to coerce this woman to have a sexual relationship with me. After I did become a Christian, she had no more reservations about being with me, and we lived together as if we were married for two years.

Today, I no longer experience same-sex attraction at all.

I pursued growth in my Christian faith, and it began to change me and the way I viewed life. I reached a point where I felt that it wasn't healthy for me to pursue lesbian relationships anymore. So eventually, my girlfriend and I broke up.

I began pursuing relationships with women who were safe and who accepted me where I was, even with my complete lack of understanding of how to relate appropriately to women. They helped me learn how to have real, healthy relationships. Now I love the world of women; it's my favorite place to be. I love to lead, teach and encourage women, and my relationships are extremely different from before. Today, I no longer experience same-sex attraction at all.

Two years after breaking up with my girlfriend, I married my husband. We have been married now for 36 years. We have five children together, and the youngest is 19.

"

I'm no longer in a place of hopelessness, shame, and regret. Instead, I feel happiness, fulfillment, and acceptance.

JONATHAN HACKER

I grew up as a pastor's kid and, therefore, spent a lot of time in church. As a kid, I didn't have many friends and found myself always searching for attention and acceptance. At an early age, I was molested by a man close to our family. As a result, I learned some things that would forever affect me. I dated girls as I went through middle school and high school, but I also experimented with friends who were guys.

At the age of 19, I started dating a girl I thought was "the one," but she ended up breaking my heart. I made a vow to never be hurt again by a woman. That is when I started dating guys and felt that I was getting more attention and acceptance. I thought that my parents wouldn't love or accept me because of the life that I chose, so I moved to Atlanta, where I started using and selling meth.

For the next few years, I was sex trafficked into the gay adult entertainment industry by people I trusted and called friends. They were seeking better drug prices. At this point, my life was out of control. I was arrested multiple times and found myself potentially facing a sentence of up to ten years in prison. But because of God and a praying community, I received a court order to go to a place called No Longer Bound, which is a trauma healing ministry. There I found God again. I always thought I was too far gone and had done too much stuff to ever be forgiven. But, the guilt and shame fell away, and love and acceptance came. I discovered my own worth, and I learned how to forgive the people who had hurt me in the past. I was able to move on.

I really didn't have anyone when I first decided to change my life. All I had was my faith. My church was a big support, and sharing with others also made me stronger. It seems that the hardest thing to do is to truly trust God. But, He did have a plan for my life.

My life now is awesome. God brought me out of that 13-year destructive lifestyle and conquered my meth addiction. I'm no longer in a place of hopelessness, shame, and regret. Instead, I feel happiness, fulfillment, and acceptance. I have been married to my wife for nine years and have two sons and a daughter. Currently, I am on the board of Fearless Identity where we are helping churches reach the LGBTQ community through biblical truths and the love of Jesus.

JONATHAN HACKER

FEARLESS IDENTITY
fearlessidentity.co

BEFORE

TODAY

ANNE EDWARD

ANNE WITH HER SONS

RESTORED HOPE NETWORK
restoredhopenetwork.org

"

The contrast of my life as a free-to-be-me lesbian and as a new woman in Christ Jesus is incomparable.

ANNE EDWARD

"You are tough on the outside, but a cream puff on the inside," my sister's friend told me in high school. How very true that statement was.

There were many reasons for that exterior shell—mainly hurt, insecurity, and loss from interpersonal relationships—so only a few would be allowed in. Later, I knew that the hurt and this defensive maneuver contributed enormously to my lesbian feelings. I craved letting another inside that protective barrier, and my need for a safe, tender, and strong female easily became sexualized. I did not know how to have safe, interdependent friendships with trustworthy others, or how to be that trustworthy friend myself.

In college, I pursued the idea of finding my female soulmate, all the while experiencing increasing emotional and mental distress. I had thrown God out of the equation as an inconvenient idea that got in the way of my goals. My lack of boundaries further eroded my sense of well-being and created a seemingly endless dark abyss in my life.

Amazingly, God had not discarded me. In my first year at university, I began to have dreams that included Jesus. I was amazed and shocked, and though I had grown up in a nominal Christian home, this was unprecedented. It happened during the period when I was going to gay bars and had joined the college women's rugby team. I had not found the "woman of my dreams" yet; instead, Jesus kept showing up.

I had not found the "woman of my dreams" yet; instead, Jesus kept showing up.

Sophomore year, I was asking important questions about truth claims and who Jesus said He was, the big picture of eternity, why there was evil in the world if God existed, and much more. What I did not expect was to join an "Evangelism Training" class where they were discussing these questions! Fully engaged, I pretended to fit in quietly as they discussed, "If we are all from primordial sludge and there is no God, why are we offended by the existence of evil?" My viewpoints were not cohesive, but Christianity offered a cohesive and reliable view of the most important topics. During the last class, we stopped the discussion and prayed. God showed me that He was there—full of kindness and authority—though He was not in my life personally. After talking with the pastor, I asked Jesus to be my Lord and Savior later that night.

What did I experience immediately? Many burdens rolled off my shoulders and I felt lighter. Joy and peace filled my heart. My eyes sparkled. I felt loved and wanted. This was the beginning of a new life with the constant companionship of God Himself through the Holy Spirit. Not that all would be easy in the years ahead, but I would have a faithful companion.

The contrast of my life as a free-to-be-me lesbian and as a new woman in Christ Jesus is incomparable. The latter is still matchless despite life's challenges and has also made me into a trustworthy woman and friend, wife, and mother.

"

My faith gave me courage to confront the wounds of my past. As I have embraced and loved myself as a man, a husband, and father, same-sex feelings have dwindled.

DANIEL MINGO

The second of seven children, I never developed a good relationship with my father. He was into sports, and I was drawn to creative, artistic, and musical outlets. Though I tried, my athletic abilities fell short, and my peers made sure to capitalize on my weaknesses. I was ridiculed by both the neighborhood kids and my own father for not fitting in with my peers. Once I began to attend public school, fitting in was even more challenging. Finding it hard to connect with other boys because of my interest in the arts, I found that most of my friends were girls.

One day at age 13, I was molested by a stranger on my way home from school. For years the secret festered in my heart, and to cope with the memory, I played the blame game, pointing at myself, God, and even my own dad because he was absent that day. As if on cue, some friends in my neighborhood then introduced me to pornography. Both the sexual abuse as an adolescent and the exposure to pornography as a teenager birthed unwanted feelings of same-sex attractions (SSA) as I entered adulthood.

When I met Jesus at age 17, I expected my life issues and painful past to be resolved, but nothing changed. So, I reluctantly and secretly acted on my SSA, while constantly seeking a way out. I never considered myself to be gay, so when I married and had children, I hoped to be finally released from my secret bondage. Sadly, I was unfaithful to my wife and absent from my family as my desires compelled me, and my untold secrets slowly crushed me. Though I didn't realize it as it was happening, I had become addicted to anonymous sexual encounters with men. I tried unsuccessfully numerous times to stop but could never seem to gain any traction with long-term results. I developed a ritual of acting out on business trips, and part of that ritual was crying out to God for forgiveness, begging Him after each episode to take these attractions away. Finally, God spoke to me, saying, "I cannot take away from you what I did not give you. You must surrender it to me." In that moment, I realized trying to quit something is not the same as surrendering it to Him. With that revelation, the Lord showed me I needed recovery from the addiction I'd given myself to for nearly 30 years. After much prayer, I confessed to my wife, telling her all about my childhood trauma, sexual abuse, and adultery. Met with love and understanding, I was empowered to go into recovery for sexual addiction. As I brought my hidden sin into the light, what was once a heavy burden was replaced with peace. Slowly but surely, our marriage was repaired through consistent honesty, ongoing confession, and trust. We've remained together for 40 years, raising three sons. What's more, last year marked 30 years since I've had any sexual contact with anyone but my wife.

I believe my faith gave me courage to confront the wounds of my past. Over time, I built relationships with men that redeemed the distorted ways I understood myself and brought healing to the traumas of molestation and perceived childhood abandonment. As I have embraced and loved myself as a man, a husband, and father, same-sex feelings have dwindled. I feel fulfilled and whole, and my former sexual desires no longer dominate my life. In 2003 I began ministering to Christians desiring freedom from unwanted attractions, and that ministry continues today.

DANIEL MINGO

ABBA'S DELIGHT, Inc.
abbasdelight.com

DEBORA BARR

DBARR MINISTRIES / *dbarrministries.org*

"

As I would see things in the Bible, I began to apply them to my life; God was transforming me from the inside out.

DEBORA BARR

Growing up, I was a bit of a tomboy. Uninterested in girly things, I enjoyed playing softball, working on cars, and building things with my father. During my teen years, I experienced a deeply hurtful betrayal by a boyfriend and a family member that initiated a season of depression, substance abuse, and suicidal ideation. During this time, I also turned away from God and began to experience feelings of same-sex attraction. In college, after being sexually harassed and assaulted by two different men, I began to dress in a more masculine way to avoid attracting the attention of men.

After college, I went into the Army to serve as a helicopter pilot, and shortly thereafter, I entered my first lesbian relationship. When God drew me back into relationship with Him, I had lived for 18 years as a lesbian and had been in three different long-term relationships. Had God not nudged me to return to church with my partner in 2003, my life may have continued on that trajectory. But after participating in a small-group study using *The Purpose-Driven Life* by Rick Warren, I felt prompted to surrender my life to Jesus. I was baptized that November, but the change in my sexual orientation had not yet occurred.

Hungry for the truth, I delved into Scripture and began reading it daily. As I would see things in the Bible, I began to apply them to my life; God was transforming me from the inside out. The more I studied, the more I fell in love with Jesus.

Two years later, God convicted me and my partner that living as lesbians was sin, and not God's best for our lives. We both made the decision to walk away from lesbianism. One of the Scriptures that I stood on during that time was Luke 9:23: "Then he [Jesus] said to them all: 'Whoever wants to be my disciple must deny themselves and take up their cross daily and follow me.'" I realized I wanted Jesus more than I wanted my old life.

The transformation took about five years from the time I walked away from that last relationship, but little by little, I began to feel like the woman God created me to be instead of the masculinized person I had become. As I began to look and act more feminine, I slowly became more comfortable with men being attracted to me, until I eventually found I liked it. I was aided in my transformational journey by Bible study with women in my church in West Virginia and books like *A Strong Delusion* by Joe Dallas and *Out of Egypt* by Jeanette Howard.

My life couldn't be more different today. I love being a woman, and I'm even attracted to men. I know who I am and whose I am. God created me with a purpose, and after straying away from God for so many years, I am now fulfilling my purpose by leading and equipping others in ministry as an associate pastor at my church. I earned a Master of Divinity in 2020 and am currently pursuing my Doctor of Ministry degree. Before that, I wrote discipleship materials and created a ministry based on how God worked in my life.

Today I am secure in who God created me to be and do not concern myself with what others think about the way I dress or how I look. God created me uniquely, and I aim to please Him above all others. I have such peace knowing that I am a child of the Most High God and that nothing can separate me from His love.

"

I also received much healing prayer over many years for the various traumas I'd experienced in my life. Today, I'm very secure in my womanhood.

DEE BARNES

I grew up the oldest of three children in a happy family. Mom was home, and my dad worked faithfully. Though we would have said we were Christians, no one in our home really knew God. A tomboy at heart, I felt very disconnected from girly things. While my friends enjoyed playing with dolls, babysitting or wearing makeup, I preferred sports. I was, in fact, a very confident and talented athlete. When it came to matters of femininity, however, I was very insecure. Wearing dresses felt stressful and uncomfortable, and I had trouble connecting emotionally with the women in my family. If I'd been a young girl living in today's society, I would have easily identified as trans because I felt much more comfortable in boy clothes.

Tragically, around age 15, I was molested by a man in my neighborhood, and this event altered the trajectory of my life. Driving me to further disconnect from the feminine, the molestation also kick-started a season of sexual promiscuity with boys and an addiction to pornography. Then, after having an abortion at age 19, I became emotionally enmeshed with a married woman with whom I began a sexual relationship. This relationship was my introduction to lesbianism, and because it felt so right, I believed the lie that I must be gay.

For the next five years, I lived in and out of relationships with other women. However, when I turned 26, I began to question my lifestyle when an attractive woman who played in my adult soccer league encouraged me to read Romans 1. A lesbian herself for 15 years, she was also a Christian, and she believed the way we were living was wrong. For the first time, I felt a sense of conviction in my spirit as the words of Scripture began to penetrate my heart. Though I had been baptized at age 15, I knew I didn't know God in the way my friend did, so I began to visit various churches in search of truth. The more I learned, the more I felt convicted. As if blinders were removed from my eyes, I could see how unhealthy and dysfunctional my life relationships had become.

Six months later, and after experiencing yet another rejection, I knelt by my bed alone one night and cried out to God. "Lord, I am sick of this," I prayed. "Please, whatever it takes, get me out." The next morning, I visited a random church alone, and for the first time, I heard a message of repentance. Responding to the altar call, I repented and surrendered my life to Jesus and was born again.

In the following weeks, I found a counselor who eventually introduced me to the Living Waters program. For the next five years, I journeyed into healing in this Christ-centered community where I was accepted and discipled. Beyond Living Waters, I also received much healing prayer over many years for the various traumas I'd experienced in my life. Today, I'm very secure in my womanhood. God gave me a wonderful husband and three amazing children, two boys and a girl, who are all now young adults. I absolutely love being a wife and mother. Currently, I am the CEO of my family's metal stamping manufacturing company. I am also the founder of His Wonderful Works ministry, where I have the privilege of helping others walk out healing from LGBTQ through lay counseling, healing prayer, and teaching at churches and local conferences.

DEE BARNES

HIS WONDERFUL WORKS, INC.
hiswonderfulworks.com

PURE HEART MINISTRIES
pureheart.rest

DONNA COLE

"

No one had ever told me God loved *me*, but suddenly, He was telling me Himself. When I walked out of that church, my life dramatically changed.

DONNA COLE

WIFE TO TOM / PAGE 143

The second of three girls, I always felt my dad had wished I was a boy. Consequently, I rejected my femininity at an early age as I tried to be the son I assumed he wanted. Like most tomboys, I preferred boyish activities and toys and even asked my friends to call me Charlie. My home life was not good. My parents' relationship was very broken, creating even more insecurity in my life. Though my dad was a good provider, he was very abusive. In addition to beating my mom, he over-disciplined us. When I was eight, they divorced, and my mother remarried a man who was even more abusive than my dad had been. When that marriage ended, she married a third time, and that stepfather molested my sisters and me. With each hurt, the walls around my heart grew thicker. "I won't be weak like my mother," I pledged. "No man will do to me what I saw done to her."

Searching for identity, I came out as a lesbian at age 18. With my mom's acceptance, I plunged into the gay lifestyle for four years only to find emptiness. I drank and took drugs in an attempt to cover the pain and fill the deep void within my heart. That's when I began to earnestly question God: *What is life about? Is Jesus real? Why church?* I truly wanted to know God, and amazingly, He responded to my prayers. About a month later, on Good Friday, I convinced my mom to go to church. Because we were Catholic and only went sporadically, she was surprised. When we walked in, a sad feeling enveloped me. But then, when I looked at the empty wooden cross up front, God miraculously gave me an open vision. As if a television screen dropped before my face, I could actually see Jesus dying on the cross! *I can't share this*, I thought. *Mom will think I am crazy or on drugs.* In that moment, God answered all my questions from the prior month: *Jesus is real! It isn't about church; He is what life is all about!* We went forward to kneel before the cross, and I began to cry as God's love washed over me. Then I heard these words: "You've looked everywhere else for love, but I love you and died for your sins." No one had ever told me God loved *me*, but suddenly, He was telling me Himself. When I walked out of that church, my life dramatically changed. Never again did I drink or do drugs, and in that moment, I knew I wasn't a lesbian anymore! Though I occasionally struggled with temptation, in my core, I knew same-sex attraction no longer defined me. Within six months to a year, my desires had completely changed.

A few years after coming to Christ, I met my husband, who also came out of homosexuality. Two very broken people, we still needed God's love and transformation in so many areas. As we journeyed into healing, we grew together in our relationship with God and each other. Today, almost 40 years later, I see myself so differently from the scared little self-protective girl I once was. I have so much hope and fulfillment, and I see womanhood as a gift. My husband and I have four grown children and seven grandchildren, which is such a miracle. We've even written a book based on the Beatitudes that helps those who need emotional healing to identify where they do not see God accurately. Just as He did for us, God wants to restore His children everywhere.

“

[An older man] lavished attention on me, and I loved it. But after a few times together, he seemed to lose interest in me. I found it difficult to enter into a long-term relationship with other men.

TOM COLE

HUSBAND TO DONNA / PAGE 140

I was the third son in a family of six children. My parents had been hoping for a girl. From the time I was very young, my mother told me that if I had been a girl, my name would have been Debbie, and this influenced how I thought of myself. My lack of interest in contact sports alienated me from the other boys in the neighborhood. When we lined up to pick teams, I would be chosen last and it was not uncommon for someone to remark, “Oh no, we got stuck with Cole. He's a sissy.” I was frequently called names like *fag, queer* or *sissy*.

I had no friends who were boys. Then an older boy in the neighborhood began to show me attention. I was elated! But one day when we were playing in his backyard, he led me into his tent. As he sexually molested me, I felt fear, revulsion, and the need to get away. At about age 12, I began to experiment sexually with other boys in the neighborhood. One neighbor and I began an eleven-year physical relationship.

In college, I majored in music and drama. I joined a vocal jazz ensemble and met a male singer who was “out of the closet” with homosexuality. One day I asked if he would take me to a gay bar, and he readily agreed. I felt fear and excitement as I anticipated the experience. I was 19 years old, but most people thought I looked 14 or 15. When we entered the bar, I noticed that many of the men were staring at me. I felt like an animal on display in the zoo. But I also loved the attention. I met an older man and we planned a date for the following week. He lavished attention on me, and I loved it. But after a few times together, he seemed to lose interest in me. I found it difficult to enter into a long-term relationship with other men.

Soon after, I met a woman at work named Rosie who constantly talked about a personal relationship with Jesus. One night she said, “My husband and I are praying for you.” I was shocked. “You pray for me?” I asked. “Yes,” she said. “We pray for you every night.” As she was leaving, she added, “Tom, I want you to know something else. I love you.” Something broke inside; the love of God reached out through Rosie and touched my heart. I hid my head under a counter, pretending to clean, while I wept. I went to church with Rosie and her family the next Sunday and gave my life to Christ!

I began telling people of my life before Christ and asking for their prayers. I felt freedom through being transparent and real about my struggles. Then I met Donna, a former lesbian, at a prayer meeting and we began a prayer partnership. After two years of studying the Bible and praying with Donna, I knew my feelings for her were more than friendship. Soon Donna and I were dating. Two months later, we were married. Our first year of marriage was torture as my insecurities poured out. But I persevered through the trials and temptations and continued to work through my deep-seated issues. Slowly, but surely, I found freedom! Today, we travel the world sharing the hope that lies in Jesus Christ. When we're at home, we get to love on our wonderful children and grandchildren.

TOM COLE

PURE HEART MINISTRIES
pureheart.rest

WAYNE BLAKELY

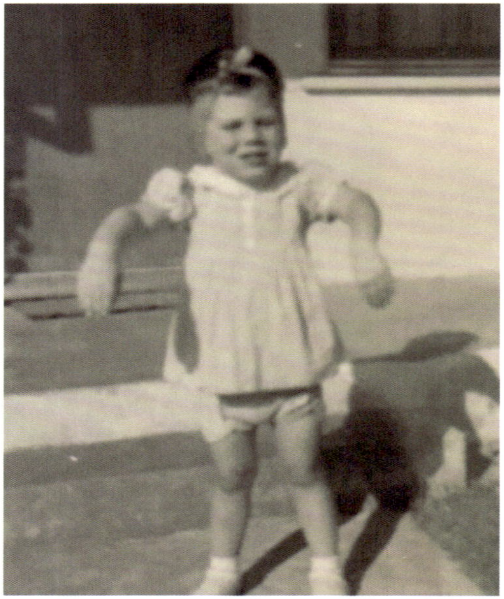

KNOW HIS LOVE MINISTRIES
knowhislove.org

"

None of the many psychologists, pastors, and teachers who tried to help me knew what to do or how to address the impact of my broken family on my identity.

WAYNE BLAKELY

My mother had always hoped for a girl, so when I was born, her disappointment was tangible. She probably would have jumped at the opportunity if allowed to leave the hospital without me. My father wasn't present to protect me in my early years because he was on assignment in the military. Unfortunately, in his absence, my mother began to physically abuse me when I was just a small child. Unable to bond with her safely and appropriately, I developed disruptive and disturbing behaviors and was eventually removed from her care. Passed around to aunts and uncles, I experienced varying degrees of instability and rejection which affected the formation of my identity. At three years old, I remember running around the house screaming, "I don't want to be a boy!" Grabbing scarves and heels and playing with dolls, I began to over-identify with the feminine.

My faith defines my identity.

Thankfully, my aunt and uncle permanently adopted me, but by the time I entered Christian school, I was frequently harassed and bullied. For 12 years, I was ridiculed for the myriad of behaviors I exhibited at school. None of the many psychologists, pastors, and teachers who tried to help me knew what to do or how to address the impact of my broken family on my identity. Nor did I know how to communicate my needs. I had a single appointment with a licensed counselor, for example, and all he did was encourage me to participate in masculine sports.

By the time I was in high school, the rejection I'd experienced from my male peers had made me crave relationships with men. I felt continuously starved for male attention, so strong feelings were sparked within me any time any boy showed interest in me, and I would then sexualize that relationship.

I left my Christian roots behind at 18 years old and lived in the gay communities of San Francisco, Key West, Portland, and Seattle. Those groups welcomed me unlike anyone ever had. Up to that point, I had been ridiculed and rejected all my life, so I never formed lasting or trustworthy friendships with men. By contrast, entering the gay community provided an opportunity for belonging. Jumping from relationship to relationship, I sought stability and intimacy. I also used every drug possible, throwing away all my standards for morality and self-dignity. AIDS would eventually claim all of my friends. None of my male friends saw the age of 50.

Because I was living in a way that I believed didn't honor God, I began to question the point of life. *Where will this end?* I wondered. Eventually, I asked God what He wanted from me. He answered, "Intimacy." So, I chose to get to know Him, court Him, and agree with Him. I trusted Him to somehow bring me wholeness, and He did.

Through years of devotion to Him, I also began to understand my childhood traumas and their implications for my life and identity. Counseling, added to my strong belief in God's ways, gave me value, purpose, and meaning. In turn, these revelations have enabled me to support others who have walked a similar path. I love to share the wholeness that I've found in Jesus. My faith defines my identity, not my temptations and desires. While I still experience same-sex attraction, I will never trade the peace I have. I live a fulfilling and joyful life.

“

Through the Holy Spirit and counseling, I addressed root issues of shame, trauma, rejection, and abuse in my life.

GEORGE CARNEAL

I was a first-grader with a secret. Same-sex attraction. There was no one for me to confide in back then in the 1970s. My father was a good man, a Baptist minister with a true desire to save the lost. Married to ministry, he was often absent from our home. I could not confide in him. My classmates were particularly cruel toward me because I was different from the other boys. Church folks weren't much nicer. They taught me that even God hated homosexuals.

I started using drugs and drinking in high school as a way of fitting in. Then, when I turned 18, I embraced gay identity and culture. Over the next 25 years, drugs, alcohol, sex, and the study of the occult and New Age teachings became ways for me to numb my pain as I searched for answers. For years I was suicidal, depressed, and addicted to my vices.

When I was around 43 years old, I cried out to God. I did not believe that He loved me, but I was desperate. So I rededicated my life to Jesus Christ, joined a loving church, and was baptized. In that moment, all the mental torment left me. I was immediately at peace with myself and certain of my right-standing with God—who spoke these words to me: “You and I are good.” That is when my journey truly began.

I am confident and secure in who I am.

Over the following years, through the Holy Spirit and counseling, I addressed root issues of shame, trauma, rejection, and abuse in my life. Hearing the stories of other formerly gay-identified people was also a major help. The process of going back to my original design was painful but necessary to stop my destructive patterns of thinking and behavior.

Today, I am convinced that God loves me, and I know Him as a Father and friend. I am changed. He is the center of my attention. I live to please Him, not others. My passion is to invite others to have a personal relationship with Christ and to help people out of the bondage that I was in.

GEORGE CARNEAL

FROM QUEER TO CHRIST
Author
georgecarneal.com

IVAN SANTOS

CHANGED MOVEMENT
changedmovement.com

"

He took the decades of depression and gave me a life worth living. Today, I have normal, healthy attractions to women.

IVAN SANTOS

I was age five when my mother became a born-again Christian and began taking us to church. I loved learning about Jesus. I felt the presence of God in times of prayer and in worship environments, and I participated with my family and friends in fellowship and Bible studies. However, around the time my family began our faith journey, I started having sexual experiences with boys my age and older. This behavior continued until age 11, when I realized that what I was doing was wrong. From that point on, a deep sense of shame and guilt consumed my thoughts, eventually leading to severe depression and suicidal ideation by age 13. My same-sex attractions were reinforced by the discovery of pornography and masturbation, and by the time I was a junior in high school, I felt like being gay was my true identity. After coming out, I continued to attend church and pursued freedom without much success. At age 22, I completely walked away from the church.

[Jesus] began to show me what it meant to be a son.

Initially, I felt freedom; I could finally be my true self. I found friends who felt like family in the LGBTQ community and pursued sexual relationships with men. Yet, I found myself self-medicating with alcohol and drugs to suppress feelings of self-hatred and hopelessness. I also continued to entertain suicidal thoughts. Though I had rejected my faith, my mother continued to pray and fast for me. She was always respectful and loving to any partners or friends I brought home, extending the love of God to them and to me. Still, she would often say things like, "I think God has a different plan for you; I think one day you will marry a woman." Irritated by her words, I believed my sexuality was fixed.

In my early thirties, my life got much worse. My drug use escalated, and I fell into escorting. At my lowest point, I cried out to God, "I don't know how my life got to this point." Miraculously, I heard Him reply: "I'm ready to show you how good life can be if you follow Me." Through the tears, I surrendered and said *yes* to Him. But what happened next was truly transformational. Several days after crying to the Lord, I had another spiritual experience with God that lasted for six consecutive days. This encounter confirmed the existence of hell, demons, Satan, heaven, and angels, and I saw God as a triune being. In addition to allowing me to experience His marvelous love, God showed me He was more powerful than the enemy, and He filled me with His Spirit. On day five, Jesus Himself came to me and told me I was cleansed. Though I was instantly freed from my addictions, I still wasn't convinced my sexuality could change. But as I chose to surrender my sexuality to Jesus, He began to show me what it meant to be a son and to walk in purity.

I soon plugged into a healthy church where I was surrounded with godly men who embraced me and modeled healthy masculinity. As I read the Bible, I began to see the beauty in God's design for man to be with woman, and as I partnered with that truth, I saw the shift in my own attractions. I have been walking with the Lord since November 2017, and my life is overflowing with joy. He took the decades of depression and gave me a life worth living. Today, I have normal, healthy attractions to women, and I no longer lust after or sexualize men. I look forward to having a wife and family one day. There is no better life than one lived in surrender to Jesus.

"

My surrender was the beginning of a transformational, intimate, and abiding relationship with Christ and His Spirit.

JASON MAXWELL

As the youngest of three boys, I often found myself feeling alone and rejected by my brothers and male peers. I struggled to make friends with other boys but found it easy to connect with girls. I was sexually abused as a child, and I remember, as a very young boy, desiring sexual intimacy and being aroused by guys on TV, in magazines, and occasionally in real life. My teenage years were particularly difficult because, while I wanted to have a girlfriend, I experienced feelings of rejection if I initiated anything beyond friendship.

In college, I became suicidal because I couldn't reconcile my attractions with my Christian faith and my desire to marry and have a family. Nor did I want to bring shame upon my family. When I was at the point of suicide, however, God intervened, impressing upon my heart that if I killed myself, the devil would win. Because I saw no way to escape my same-sex attractions, I took God's rescue as his approval of my desires, and I came out to my family and friends at age 19. Desiring the closest thing to a marriage and family as I could get, given my sexual attractions, I turned my attention to finding a life partner.

I eventually met a young man with whom I would spend the next 11 years. During this time, we attended an all-gay church for several years before moving on to a non-denominational church. I was focused on building a successful career, and by age 32, I owned the largest home staging and design company in Texas. I was gay, successful, and happy by all worldly standards. With a thriving business and personal life, I wasn't looking for change.

But God had other plans for me. On May 23, 2010, I had a radical experience of God, who poured His love into me in such a way that my life was forever changed. For the first time in my life, I experienced true love. "Are you ready to follow me now?" I heard God say. "Your eternal life is in jeopardy." Within three weeks of that experience, I walked away from my partner, started the process of closing my business, and relocated from Dallas, Texas, to Centerton, Arkansas, to begin a journey of self-discovery. Ready to do life His way, I repented of my sexual behaviors and began actively attending the church where I had my God encounter.

My surrender was the beginning of a transformational, intimate, and abiding relationship with Christ and His Spirit. For the next four months, I continually sought the Lord to understand what my new identity in Him was supposed to look like. During this time, I began to believe that I could be attracted to, fall in love with, and marry a woman. In December of 2011, I married my beautiful wife Sarah, and today, we have three amazing daughters, Hollyn, Emelyn, and Gracyn. As a family we are actively involved in our local church and homeschooling community. Being a father has changed my understanding of God, masculinity, and sonship. While many of my mannerisms and interests in art and creativity remain the same, I no longer view masculinity as something toxic to avoid. I'm blessed to have solid friendships with men who are brothers in Christ. In 2015 Sarah and I started Flames2Fire Ministries, which is dedicated to discipling those with unwanted same-sex attractions. We also serve as a resource to churches around the country to help educate leadership and parents on how to walk alongside members and kids who struggle with sexual brokenness.

JASON MAXWELL

FLAMES2FIRE MINISTRIES
flames2fire.com

JEANNETTE LEUTY

"

Christians were the people who loved me wholeheartedly and ultimately helped free me from the pain I had carried in my heart. They responded to my vulnerability with tenderness.

JEANNETTE LEUTY

A tomboy growing up, I loved to be outside, play sports, and build things. In junior high, I clearly remember the boy-crazy girls putting on makeup and fixing their hair; I wanted nothing to do with those girly things. Though I recognized I was a biological girl, I felt like a misfit who couldn't fully relate to either gender. Never attracted to men, I first noticed feelings of same-sex attraction (SSA) around age 13. But because I didn't like those feelings, I never "came out" to my family and didn't fully adopt a gay identity until I was about 20 years old.

As my SSA increased, I experienced a huge conflict between my feelings and my faith. Having been raised in a Christian home, I wanted to be obedient to the Lord. But I harbored so much shame and guilt and had no friends in whom I could confide. Afraid of further rejection, I kept all of my emotions bottled up. Battling suicidal feelings, I would often cry myself to sleep. I also turned to masturbation. When I was introduced to the LGBTQ community, however, I felt accepted and welcomed. *Finally*, I thought, *I belong*. Though all of my friends were lesbians, I didn't enter a same-sex relationship until my mid-twenties. Shortly thereafter, I began to recognize the brokenness in others as well as myself. There was always a hunger for more: more love, more acceptance, more intimacy, more inclusion. It felt as if we were overcompensating for what was lacking. Life began to feel hopeless. I had a longing in my heart to draw closer to God, but not knowing that he was the fulfillment of all that was lacking, I sought comfort in other women. Eventually, however, I began to feel stuck in my current relationship. The Lord began wooing my heart, yet I was afraid to give up the friendship, love, and companionship I so desperately needed. But the Lord did not give up on me.

I was working as a firefighter when one day our engine was dispatched to check on a fire that had been put out the day before. I was riding in the back with another firefighter when we collided with a logging truck. As if in slow motion, the engine tumbled up and over and caught fire. Gripped with fear, I cried out to the Lord asking for forgiveness for my sins. After the incident, I began to reevaluate my life. I knew it was ridiculous to think I could keep living for myself and expect God's blessing. I knew I needed the Lord, and I knew I needed to end my same-sex relationship. Though it took me a while to leave the relationship, when I did, I zealously pursued the Lord.

I sought out passages in the Bible to ease my wounded heart; I found different resources online, got connected with a Bible study, started attending a prayer group and church. For a long time, the church had been where I felt most rejected and ashamed. Christians seemed to have the biggest problem with how I lived my life. Yet, unbelievably, the church became the place where most of my emotional healing happened. Christians were the people who loved me wholeheartedly and ultimately helped free me from the pain I had carried in my heart. They responded to my vulnerability with tenderness.

God continues to bring people into my life who are willing to walk the journey with me and give me the space I need to authentically and truthfully share my heart and my life. Leaving LGBTQ and embracing myself as a woman has caused me to feel healthier and more fulfilled than ever before.

"

I thought because of my choices God had abandoned me, but instead I discovered He had never left.

JESSICA OWENS

Raised in a Christian family, I always had an awareness of God. As a girl growing up in the South, I believed Jesus loved me, and I wanted to serve Him. However, as an early adolescent, I had an unwanted sexual encounter with a boy, which caused confusion and shame. After that, I began struggling with new sexual temptations but told no one about this sexual abuse. In high school, I was the athletic girl who didn't enjoy "girly" things like makeup, dresses, or shopping. Guys didn't invite me to school dances, so I believed that I wasn't beautiful enough to be pursued. I was a teenager impacted by insecurities around my beauty.

In college, my insecurities grew, and I often experienced anxiety and fear. I found myself needing others' approval and affirmation to feel satisfied and to confirm that I belonged among my peers. I became codependent in friendships and easily experienced rejection. At 19, I began to experience same-sex attraction, which was confusing. However, as I found comfort in friendships within the LGBTQ community, I began to adopt these feelings as an identity. Acting on my newly discovered feelings, I began living a double life. I was the "good Christian girl" when I was with my family but a different person around my peers. I binged on alcohol and had sex to cope with the internal pain and confusion I was experiencing. In truth, I longed for a committed, intimate relationship to validate my identity.

After living as a closeted lesbian for six years, I met some married, heterosexual couples who seemed to have a joy and peace that I was missing. As a result, I began attending a church regularly in 2012. One day, as a boy was being baptized, I heard God say to me: "Jessica, don't you want your father to see your children be warriors for My Kingdom?'" Even though I was sitting with my girlfriend, this statement pierced my heart and illuminated my true identity. I thought because of my choices God had abandoned me, but instead I discovered He had never left. Deep down I knew I wanted to serve God and to raise a family. Afterward, I called my mom and explained to her what I'd been going through. She responded with compassion and unconditional love, which then gave me the courage to share with a minister at church the following Sunday. Met with love once again, I thought, "How could God love me this much after all I have done?" During the worship service that day, I experienced what I can only describe as the power of God resting on me. In that moment, I dedicated my life to Him. Miraculously, following this moment, I no longer experienced attraction to women, struggled with masturbation, or desired to binge drink to cope with my pain. God became my comforter and friend. I left many old relationships behind and trusted Him to give me new friendships, which He faithfully did.

How could God love me this much?

My involvement in Christian activity—attending church weekly, being involved in women's small groups, finding places to serve in my church and in my community, times of prayer, and pastoral counseling—have all been key to my journey of wholeness. God has done so much in my life that today I am a licensed pastor. Confident in my femininity, I love the woman I have become. I no longer experience overwhelming fear in my friendships with women or men, but rather have learned how to have healthy, meaningful relationships with both sexes. My life is full of joy, peace, and hope!

JESSICA OWENS

CHANGED MOVEMENT
changedmovement.com

LEON JONCK

CHANGED MOVEMENT
changedmovement.com

"

Today, I feel a long-lasting, inner peace that I know only comes from God.

LEON JONCK

As a young boy, I felt like something was missing. Though I didn't identify as LGBTQ, I struggled with same-sex attraction and questioned whether I would ever be able to be authentic with someone else or overcome my attraction to men. I often battled suicidal thoughts and depression. Alcohol and porn became my way of coping with the pain of isolation and loneliness.

As a teenager, I acted out on my feelings toward men and, as a result, experienced fear of rejection from family and friends. I started living a double life, pretending I was okay on the outside but crumbling on the inside.

In my late twenties, I completed an Alpha Course, which is a place for people who want to explore Christianity and ask questions. A lady in the course asked the pastor what he would do if someone who had SSA came to the church. The pastor told her that he would love and support them, just like he would anyone else. For the first time I realized it was possible that I could be loved and not rejected by God because of my struggles.

Born again and baptized a year later, I began to share my story with others. Over the next five years, I embarked on a journey of surrendering my sexuality to God. Though my confidence in my new identity sometimes wavered, God always came through for me with remarkable reminders that he was guiding me. In 2018, for instance, I had a powerful spiritual experience one night during a worship service; when I awoke the next day, I heard the phrase, "You are free!" resounding in my head. I instantly knew what God was saying to me: I would no longer be a slave to my desires. Overjoyed, I began learning how to renew my mind with truth and live as Christ's new creation.

Then again in 2019, I was lying on the floor one day when I had a vision of Jesus coming and kneeling next to me. I watched as He pulled my spine out through my brain, and it looked like a bunch of loose wires. He said, "We are going to rewire your mind. It's not going to be easy, but I am going to do it with you." Because I had thought about myself a certain way for so long, I realized during this encounter that I actually needed to learn to think differently. Today, I feel a long-lasting, inner peace that I know only comes from God. I know God cares about me and my struggles, and I can see in my own life that change is possible. I look back with thankfulness to God for everything He has done in my life and in my heart to walk me into the freedom I experience today.

“

My transformation took place during a prayer vigil around my hospital bed on Easter Sunday, 2008, where I lay in a coma dying of AIDS.

MARK NELSON

I was raised in the church by faith-filled, prayerful parents. However, through multiple unwanted events and pride, the enemy took control of my life at an early age. This led to a 10-year addiction to alcohol, drugs, pornography, and unwanted homosexual feelings. In 1998, I was introduced to the gay community while attending college. By 2000, I was fully immersed in gay culture and actively involved with several LGBTQ activist groups. Five years later, I had an experience of God where I was deeply convicted by Him, but would continue to stay in a monogamous same-sex relationship for three more years. I attended a local gay church during this time and still felt controlled by my desires and full of confusion.

The Word of God is my primary resource for overcoming all things.

My transformation took place during a prayer vigil around my hospital bed on Easter Sunday, 2008, where I lay in a coma dying of AIDS. Prayerful people led by my mom and dad began to speak life over my body, meditating on Bible passages and boldly proclaiming the promises found in the Bible. I actually died at one point with my praying father watching the resuscitation efforts. I experienced death as my soul separated from my physical body, and I floated above the room and saw medical personnel working vigorously to bring me back. I quickly transitioned into God's judgment where I faced a piercing light. God showed me my sins in different scenes that were grounded in sexual sin, pride and rebellion. I was then thrown into complete darkness, where I experienced hell and its unbearable heat, head-splitting cries for help, and unending physical torment. I cried out in repentance, “Jesus!” Then I heard His voice, “I'm here.” In an instant my soul re-entered my physical body, and I witnessed, what I'll describe as the wind of the Holy Spirit enter my ICU room and remove all satanic influence in an instant. The atmosphere changed from darkness to light and chaos to peace. It was no coincidence this day was Resurrection Sunday. I experienced that there is power in the Cross of Jesus.The shed blood of Jesus became real to my life. From that moment forward, my body began to heal and my failing organs were restored. I walked out of the hospital with a new life in Christ.

In May 2008, while I was in rehabilitation, God spoke to me and said, “You will marry Beth,” my longtime friend. I did so that next November and we remain married today. Marriage has allowed me to experience masculinity through being her husband while becoming a part of her family of three sons, a daughter-in-law, and five grandsons. The Word of God is my primary resource for overcoming all things. I presently serve the Lord in full-time ministry.

MARK NELSON

EXCHANGE MINISTRIES
exchangeministries.org

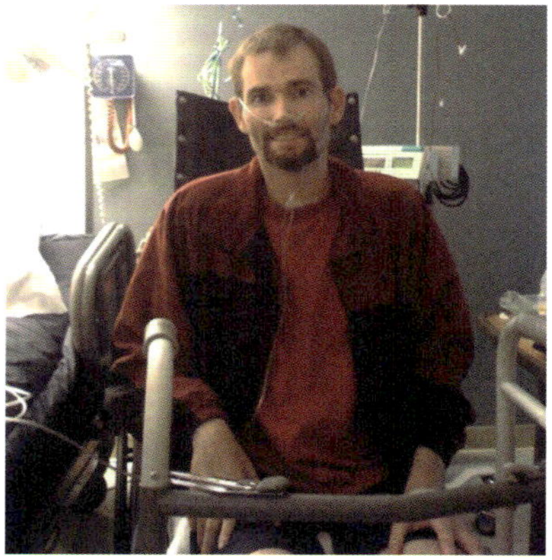

RACHEL PLYLER

HER VOICE MVMT
hervoicemvmt.com

"

Rejection ruled my life as an unrelenting symphony of lies, as I attempted every which way to gain acceptance.

RACHEL PLYLER

I knew this wasn't what God had for me, but I didn't care. Here I was again, sleeping with my best friend, who had somehow secretly become my girlfriend. I didn't know how we had gotten here or where we were going, but as I would tell God each time He convicted my heart, I really didn't care. At least someone finally loved me.

I was raised in church by two loving parents and had loved Jesus since I was a little girl. I knew I had heard Him call me into ministry at 15 years old and tell me I would see revival. Even though I believed Him, I couldn't escape the lie that I wasn't lovable. Rejection ruled my life as an unrelenting symphony of lies, as I attempted every which way to gain acceptance.

So when my best friend and I went on a trip our senior year of high school and innocently ended up sharing a bed, the enemy stepped right in to twist it. The more it progressed, the more I pushed away the conviction in my heart and believed finally someone loved me, even if it was a same-sex relationship.

The shame and the thrill were simultaneously overwhelming. God would call to me as I lay in her bed awake. I would push Him away in the night but the next day preach His name as a youth leader and a ministry student.

Inside I felt empty, not fulfilled like I had hoped. Darkness overtook me even after the relationship ended. I spiraled into depression and anxiety. I thought I had escaped the lie, but I was alone, stuck, hopeless, and purposeless. I had lost track of who I was and didn't like who I had somehow become. A spirit of death and suicide taunted me to just die.

Instead of judgment, I was met with real love.

But God was chasing down my heart. Slowly, I started to encounter God's love in a new way and I was coming alive again. I moved to Portland and determined to start over, pretend this never happened, pursue Jesus, and never look back.

But I couldn't outrun my secrets and my brokenness. And same-sex attraction, depression, and rejection followed me. This time, though, I encountered a community of people alive in the Holy Spirit, who started to walk with me through freedom and learning to be vulnerable. I got freedom in so many areas, but when God asked to walk with me through the same-sex attraction, I ran the other way into a masturbation and pornography addiction. I couldn't fathom telling anyone ever, the shame was so intense. I was a leader at my church, a good Christian girl but inside tormented by shame and addiction.

I'll never forget the Sunday in 2017 when God gave me a clear opportunity to come clean. I found myself at the altar for prayer, when my friend leaned down in my ear and said, "Pornography, you have to go, in Jesus' name." I was confronted with a choice: keep lying and living a façade or tell the truth, risk the possibility of losing everything, but be free. I chose to come clean, exhausted from the weight of shame and lies. I told the whole truth. And in the kindness of God, instead of being met with judgment, I was met with real love that walked beside me each step of the journey to finally be free and learn to know and embrace the real me—the fierce, feminine, joyful, alive, pure, forgiven, accepted, and deeply-loved daughter!

"

Seven years after I committed my life to Jesus, my ex-partner also made a commitment to Him.

SARAH SEDGWICK

I was always what would be called a tomboy. Going to an all-girls school, I gravitated toward the sporty crowd and, as such, never seemed much different from the others. It was when I went to college and started going to gay clubs that I began to dress in a more androgynous way, with short hair and jeans and a hoodie as my go-to outfit. Wearing feminine clothing such as dresses was a big *no* for me. I had turned my back on the church as a teenager because of my same-sex attraction (SSA) and spent 30 years living as a lesbian. I had a 16-year relationship with another woman during that time.

Before I became a Christian, and before God started reaching out to me, life was good. I had friends and was actively involved in sports, and my partner and I had a very settled relationship. I had a better relationship with my family than ever before and at 48 years of age was simply getting on with life. But the reality was that I was very broken inside.

Every afternoon after work I would take the dog for a walk and listen to the radio, usually a pop station. But one day I "just happened" to tune in to a different station. Suddenly a worship song was playing. Immediately after the song's conclusion, a Joyce Meyer teaching began. I noticed she was speaking about God in ways that were unfamiliar to me. I listened to Joyce's teachings over the next few months and started learning about a God who loved me, despite my sin, and a God who wanted a relationship with me. A few months later, I walked into a church and started my journey of discovery. No one bothered me. I was given space to listen, learn, and grow. I began to see people who reflected Jesus, and that's what I wanted!

After a conversation with my partner about what it meant to be a Christian and stopping all sexual activity, I prayed and asked God's forgiveness and for Him to come into my life. There was a long journey ahead, and it took time to eventually leave my partner and fully extricate myself from my old identity. But God was gracious and walked the whole journey to freedom with me! I went through a season of thinking I was always going to identify as a celibate gay Christian. But over time that identity has dropped off me, and I no longer consider myself that way. I was encouraged by reading the Bible and other faith-based literature. There was also Christian counseling, not to address the SSA, but to address the roots of unforgiveness, abuse, and lack of self-worth which I had carried. My involvement in an amazing women's ministry and a small prayer group have also strengthened me.

God has been so good to me, and I am joyful and thankful for all that He has done, starting with the fact that seven years after I committed my life to Jesus, my ex-partner also made a commitment to Him. We remain friends, now living 300 miles apart. My attitude toward clothing has changed; my wardrobe now sports an array of clothing. Sure, there are still jeans and hoodies, but also dresses, handbags and heels!

Today, I have such a good relationship with my family, whom I had pushed away for so many years. God has replaced my old friend group with a new group of friends who not only love me but also pray for me and uplift me daily. I learn and grow in my faith daily, and my relationship with God is maturing as I continue to surrender to Him.

SARAH SEDGWICK

TRANSFORMED MINISTRIES
transformedbygodslove.com

SHERRY GURNEY

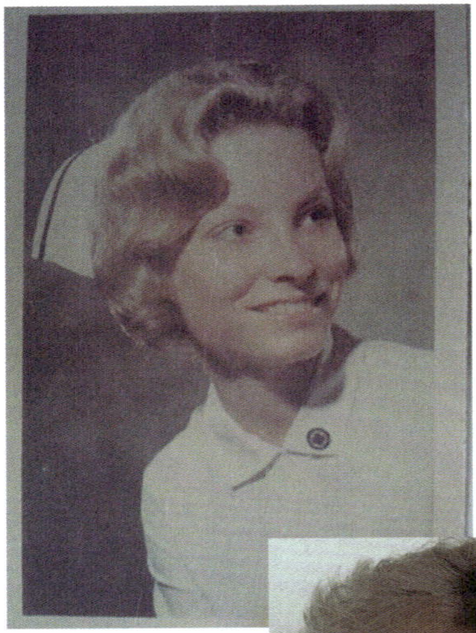

MOMS AND POPS SUPPORT GROUP
bctulsa.churchcenter.com/groups

"

I enjoy spending time with my children and grandchildren! ...They would not have been born had it not been for the mighty work of God!

SHERRY GURNEY

Raised in a chaotic, alcoholic home, I was physically abused and emotionally starved as a child. In addition to acute anxiety and maternal attachment issues, I also developed a mistrust and hatred of men. Growing up, I was embarrassed by my looks because I matured more slowly than my friends. Then, at age 16, I fell headlong in love with a friend on a Girl Scout trip. She was strong, exciting, and caring. How could this be? I had never felt this strong emotion about anyone before! When I returned home, I searched for answers in the local library and learned about homosexuality. Because my great, great grandmother had introduced me to Jesus as a child, I considered myself a Christian. So when I searched the Bible and found that God expressed strong disapproval of homosexuality, I assumed that God also hated me. Why was this happening? I was very worried and confused.

When I graduated from high school, I enrolled in an out-of-state nursing program. Relieved to be away from my hometown, I could finally be me. But who was I? As my schooling and employment opened opportunities to meet others with the same temptations, I soon walked into secret lesbian relationships. Ironically, I still held on to my Christian beliefs and served as an officer in the Nurses Christian Fellowship. But I was tortured by the fact that my double life was displeasing to God. I prayed and pleaded with God to change me.

Then, one evening in 1970, when I was 24 years old, I had a dramatic experience that set me free inside. Our church had been fasting for a week, holding meetings each evening in various homes. On this particular evening, I had come home to an empty house. As I continued praying, I heard the Lord say, "You don't trust me." I argued that I trusted Him, but not people. He asked, "Do you trust me concerning the lesbianism?" I began to cry angrily, yelling at God. "How do I know how I can trust anyone?" I exclaimed. "Babies learn to trust when they are cared for, fed, clothed, and protected. I never experienced that care!" As I wept at my bedside, I told Him I wanted to be free, but that He was going to have to teach me how to trust. That night He lifted a huge weight of fear and shame off of me and filled me with trust and love by His Spirit. I expected the same-sex attraction to be gone, but when it wasn't, I prayed to God, trusting that He knew what was needed to finish the work He began in me. I began attending Bible studies and dove into the Bible.

Upon realizing that my relationships were often codependent, I completed Celebrate Recovery's 12-Step program, eventually leading several groups myself. I also participated in one-on-one Christian cognitive therapy, which addressed more wounds from childhood. I enrolled in Bible school, and while serving as the campus nurse, I realized one day that my attractions were gone. Students were coming and sharing their pain with unwanted temptations, and I was sharing biblical truths with them, totally untriggered! During that season in school, I also met my husband with whom I went into full-time ministry, even serving overseas.

Free for 50+ years, I'm now a widow and retired, and I enjoy spending time with my children and grandchildren! I rejoice when I think that they would not have been born had it not been for the mighty work of God!

CHANGED

CHANGED

CHANGED
ONCEGAY.COM

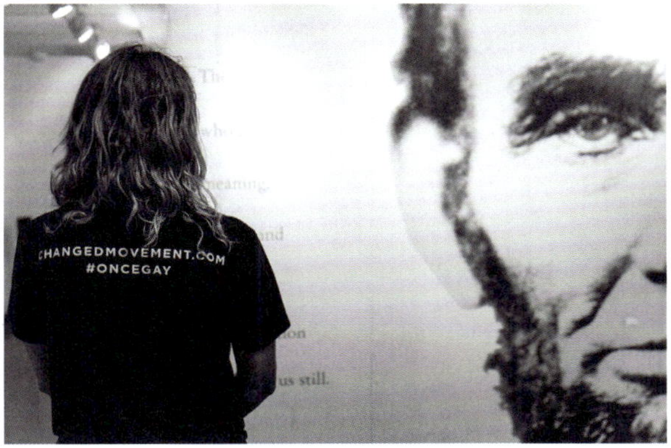
CHANGEDMOVEMENT.COM
#ONCEGAY

CHANGED

CHANGED

Rainbow
Revival

IN LOVING MEMORY
OF OUR FRIEND
MICHAEL MARTINEZ

CHANGED
CHANGED

IF THIS BOOK HAS IMPACTED YOU
OR YOU'D LIKE MORE INFORMATION,
PLEASE REACH US AT:

CHANGEDMOVEMENT.COM

JOIN THE MOVEMENT

STAY CONNECTED

/CHANGEDMVMT

SHARE YOUR STORY

SUBMIT AT **CHANGEDMOVEMENT.COM/SHARE**

POSTING ONLINE? USE **#ONCEGAY**
